BOUND FOR GLORY

THE HORATIO ALGER STORY OF FSU's BOBBY BOWDEN

BOUND FOR GLORY

By BOBBY BOWDEN
as told to MIKE BYNUM

THE WE BELIEVE TRUST FUND
at the

Bank of A&M
REPUBLIC OF TEXAS

COLLEGE STATION, TEXAS

ALSO BY MIKE BYNUM
High Tide
Bryant . . . The Man, The Myth
Never Say Quit
Aggie Pride
We Believe

Library of Congress Cataloging Number applied for

Copyright © 1980 by *The We Believe Trust Fund.*
All Rights Reserved, First Printing August, 1980

ISBN applied for

Published by
The We Believe Trust Fund
The Bank of A&M Trust Department
111 University Drive
College Station, Texas 77840

Cover Illustration: Daniel A. Moore, New Life Art, Inc.,
Birmingham, Alabama
Book Design: Drake Printers, Inc., Tuscaloosa, Alabama
Lithographed by: Rose Printing, Inc., Tallahassee, Florida

Acknowledgements

In order to be successful in attempting to write this wonderful story, there were a lot of people who gave of their time unselfishly to make this book possible. It is their efforts that we wish to applaud.

To Mr. Bill McGrotha of the *Tallahassee Democrat,* to Mr. Frank Flynn of WCTV; to Mr. Bill Sutton of The Lewis State Bank; to Mr. Frank DeBord; to Mr. Manly Neighbors; to Mr. Don Fauls; to Mr. Robert Cleckler; to Mr. John Albritton; to Mr. Andy Miller and Mr. Charlie Barnes and their Seminole Booster staff; to Dr. Bernie Sliger, to Mr. Jim Smith; to Mr. Phil Fordyce; to Mr. Ronald Weathers of the *Birmingham News;* to Mr. Mark Carlson and the Sports Information Staff at Florida State who so graciously allowed me to research their files; to Tim Rosaforte, Edwin Pope, Larry Guest, Tom McEwen, and the other great journalists who have done an excellent job in covering Florida State athletics; to The First National Bank of Tuscaloosa, Alabama; and especially to the gentlemen who stood behind us and supported our efforts.

To Mom and Dad who brought me into this wonderful game of life, and to Ann, my beautiful wife, who's been cheering for me ever since. Also, to my six wonderful children who always stood behind me, went with us through the hard times, stayed out of trouble, and in the final result turned out to be fine Christian young men and women.

The Bowden Gang—(Row 1) Daughters-in-law Twila and Linda, with Ann (middle). (Row 2, left to right) Ginger, Terry and Tommy. (Row 3, left to right) Daughter-in-law Janet, Steve, Robyn, son-in-law Jack, Jeffrey, and Coach Bowden.

The We Believe Trust

The We Believe Trust is a living memorial, in honor of the thousands of young men who have played for Coach Paul W. Bryant at Maryland, Kentucky, Texas A&M and Alabama. The primary purpose of the *We Believe Trust* will be to administer annual scholarships to the four respective universities and the money derived from book sales in that school will be used by the *We Believe Trust* to only benefit that school.

This trust is dedicated to eight young men who survived a pre-season war-camp at Junction, Texas in 1954 as well as a countless legion of others who have played for Coach Paul "Bear" Bryant. Players much like Dennis Goehring, Don Watson, Bobby Drake Keith, Bobby Lockett, Jack Pardee, Dee Powell, Gene Stallings and Lloyd Hale, who helped bring in 1956 to Texas A&M its first Southwest Conference title in fifteen years.

These men from Maryland, Kentucky, Texas A&M and Alabama learned the lessons as youngsters that would mold them into winners. It would also make them believers.

The We Believe Trust is to be administered by the Trust Department of the Bank of A&M, College Station, Texas.

Contents

Foreword

When I think of how my friend, Bobby Bowden, has taken Florida State to the top of the college football world, it so often reminds me of a similar story that took place in Green Bay, Wisconsin, in the late fifties when a bright and bubbly, yet little known, coach by the name of Vince Lombardi came to town.

Prior to the Lombardi era, the Packer's football program was at a low ebb. However, when Coach Lombardi took over, things began to change. Fast. He transformed us from one of the losingest teams in the NFL to a championship contender. And it all began with three key coaching philosophies; *enthusiasm, hard work,* and *dedication.*

It was just a matter of time before we began to *believe* in the Lombardi system. And in the years that followed, what happened is all history.

In 1976, Bobby accepted the challenge of rebuilding the losingest college football program in America. It was a difficult task, but Bobby never gave up. He just kept telling his team that "they could win." And they listened.

It's been a long trip up the road to success for FSU's Bobby Bowden. For so many years he has had to overcome the ploddings of obscurity, the low-budgeted programs and the pressures of demanding alumni. But like a true gentleman and a great coach, he stood tall. He proved that he could win—his way.

Bobby is a man of very high principles. He stands for the things I like to think I stand for. They're considered corny in the society in which we live today, because I think there's no longer enough emphasis on loyalty and respect and pride. He stands for self-sacrifice and dedication and religion, and those are values that don't get much attention anymore.

Over the years, Bobby has been a builder of quality young men as well as winning football teams. *Bound for Glory* is the testimony of that wonderful story.

July 5, 1980   Bart Starr, Head Coach
                                      Green Bay Packers

Introduction

It was a late autumn afternoon when I stumbled upon a rare, yet modestly preserved, book. Its pages were yellowed and worn, and the binding was beginning to tear at the seams. Quickly, I opened it, a work which had obviously been a literary treasure to someone, for the chapter that I turned to had previously been marked by a person unknown many, many years ago.

It read, "Again it is the ninth inning; there are two outs, the bases are full, Yale is behind 3 to 0, and Frank Merriwell is at bat. The count is three and two, and . . . ." Yes, it was a typical Merriwell finish, a proverbial expression which comes directly from the daring deeds of this greatest of heroes—the All-American.

Looking back on that day, I realize that I was able to relive the past and recapture the great American dream; for here was the America of our best myths—when it required no apology to be honest, courageous and law-abiding; when hard work was a prerequisite for success; when danger was to be confronted, not avoided; when duty was meant to be performed, not shirked. Yet, these ideals are not dead.

Today, a similar story could be told of Bobby Bowden, the happy-go-lucky, highly enthusiastic coach who in 1976 inherited a dying Florida State football program and quickly brought it from the basement of despair to the penthouse of the college ranks. According to one leading sports writer in the South, "Bobby Bowden sports a homespun personality, coaches with the daring explosiveness of a George Gipp, and week after week wins football games like Charley Conerly once did for the New York Giants."

But life has not always been so rosey for Bowden. At age 13, he was stricken by an illness that brought into doubt not only his future in football but his very life as well. Later, as a college student, he chose to leave his beloved Alabama football team for a smaller, less known school—in order to marry the woman he loved. (But that brings us again to the hero story, does it not?)

A lot can be said for this great coach who once had to get on State-wide T.V. to convince a future Florida State All-America, Ron Simmons, that he was not taking a head coaching job at Ole Miss. And what about the great humility of the man himself, who, though faced with the rising costs of maintaining a large family—he and Ann have six children—, was to pledge, "I'm giving ten percent of my salary to God, no matter how great the sacrifice!"

Once, he wanted to coach at The University of Alabama, and Bear Bryant, the head man, would have loved for the eager-to-learn Bowden to join him. Yet there was one major obstacle. Bryant explained: "Bobby, if I hire you away from Howard College, then how am I gonna face all of those upset Baptists next fall?"

Now, things are much better for FSU's Bobby Bowden. He has finally overcome the adversities and years of obscurity at lesser known schools, and, according to two FSU supporters, whose restaurants, *Brother's Three* and *Captain Anderson's*, Bowden frequently patronizes, "Life began for Bobby Bowden at 46, when he decided to come to Florida State."

I suspect that *Bound for Glory* will confirm this partisan comment, while providing the reader with an enlightening and inspirational journey, a story that "Burt Standish" would have been proud to write.

June 25, 1980

MIKE BYNUM
Tuscaloosa, Alabama

The Great Sacrifice

"I owe most everything to football, in which I have spent the greater part of my life. And I have never lost my respect, my admiration or my love for what I consider a great game. And each Saturday, after the battle, one group savors victory, another group lives in the bitterness of defeat. The many hurts seem a small price to have paid for having won, and there is no reason at all that is adequate for having lost. To the winner there is one hundred percent elation, one hundred percent laughter, one hundred percent fun; and to the loser the only thing left for him is one hundred percent resolution, one hundred percent determination. And it's a game, I think, a great deal like life in that it demands that a man's personal commitment be toward excellence and be toward victory, even though you know that ultimate victory can never be completely won. Yet it must be pursued with all of one's might. And each week there's a new encounter, each year a new challenge. But all of the rings and all of the money and all of the color and all of the display, they linger only in the memory. The spirit, the will to win and the will to excel, these are the things that endure and these are the qualities that are so much more important than any of the events that occasion them. And I'd like to say that the quality of any man's life has got to be a full measure of that man's personal commitment to excellence and to victory, regardless of what field he may be in."

Vince Lombardi

Once Upon A Time

Burt Reynolds and an army of bodyguards stood a few yards to his left. Larry Csonka stood a few yards to his right. And thousands of Seminole fans kept yelling, "Bobby! Bobby! Bobby!"

A television camera was poked in his face. And he wore enough wires to talk to NBC, his pressbox coaches, the moon, and his aunt in Birmingham.

Now, the game was over. Oklahoma 24, FSU 7. Disappointedly Bobby Bowden made his way toward the team locker room, but like a true champion his head was held high.

Oh, how difficult it must have been to travel those last few yards across the gridiron. It was a truthful moment of raw courage. For this sight, this unforgettable heartmoving sight on a lonely January 1st evening in Miami, explained in a thousand ways how the Florida State Seminoles had come so close in this monumental year, fought so hard, yet died so violently in this post-season Orange Bowl classic.

Once upon a time . . . Yes, this is that type of story—a dream-come-true fairy tale. One of those good ol' bedtime stories complete with a happy ending that Mom and Dad used to tell you when you were just a little tot. For those were the days when life was full of heroes, real tall, life-like . . . Tarzan, the Lone Ranger, Superman, and Dick Tracy.

For this one-of-a-kind story, the Bobby Bowden story, is what life in America is all about—high morals, honesty, hard work, and a true sense of fair play. Yet, Bowden's story is much more than that, for his is the Great American Dream, completely equipped with episodes from Frank Merriwell, the Bible, Babe Ruth, Abe Lincoln and Jack the Giant Killer. For without a doubt, he has become the greatest of America's Horatio Alger heroes.

In his career, Robert Cleckler Bowden has been the head coach at four schools—South Georgia College, Howard College, West Virginia University and Florida State University. At each institution he has been remarkably successful in the two most important goals in his career: Bowden has taken losing teams and made them winners, recruited immature boys and made them men.

Very few coaches can boast of a record comparable to his 129 victories and 55 defeats, and none can duplicate the unique plan for success that he has carried across the Southland: Bobby Bowden, the proclaimed Savior of FSU, has rebuilt pride and success into Seminole football. It isn't what Bowden does—but *how*. Every game is a full scale production, every session flared with special drama. And operating from the off-Broadway theater of Florida State University, he has become and will always remain, the unequaled *impressario* of our *Outdoor Stage*.

For something must be said of this muffin-faced man who sports an old-fashioned haircut, reads his Bible daily, quotes philosophies from Dr. Norman Vincent Peale, and preaches his football gospel from books authored by Billy Graham, "Bear" Bryant and George Allen. Football, the Bowden way, without a doubt, earns instant respect. Wherever you go today in the State of Florida, you will continuously hear the same response from businessmen, professors, and homemakers alike: Bobby Bowden is the *greatest*. He has a mind that touches genius, a blow-torch spirit, physical courage, infectious with rare charm. He is truly a personality once encountered, always remembered.

But if I had to pick one reason for Bowden's enormous success, it would be that he has *magnetism*—that special quality of being able to walk-in and electrify a room. His forte is making people think like *winners*, getting them to *believe* in themselves. He is a great psychologist, great at analyzing individuals, knowing which players need to be driven and which ones need a friendly pat-on-the-fanny. Bowden can put his finger on the key elements of a person's personality. He knows how to *motivate* them—what buttons to push. And to those *believers* all across America, who have since looked up to him and formed the Bobby Bowden legion, he has been affectionately deified as a man who can walk on water, a man who can do no wrong.

But what has made him the coach he is today?

First of all, Bobby Bowden believes in the Spartan life, the total self-sacrifice; and to succeed and reach the pinnacle that he has, you've got to be that way. You've got to have total dedication to the program. The hours that you put into a job cannot even be considered. The job is to be done, and if takes a thousand hours—you give it a thousand hours. If it takes thirty minutes, you give it thirty minutes.

Next, I feel that Coach Bowden is one of the finest salemen ever, a super salesman. He has a knack for selling himself, his system, and his ideas to football players and fans alike. He's been able to do this because, first, he believes passionately in what he's selling—in himself and his system. Second, he's a great teacher, both on the field and at the blackboard. The man is a perfectionist, and he is never satisfied simply by victory. He always wants each member of his team to play as well as he is capable of playing.

And the better people get to know Bobby Bowden, the more they respect him. They admire what he stands for. He's a high principled man who stands for the things America stands for. Bowden stands for self-sacrifice and loyalty, pride and dedication, respect and religion—old-fashioned values that don't get much attention anymore.

Bowden and his idol, Coach Paul "Bear" Bryant, enjoy a round of golf during 1977 Pro-Am in Orlando.

In 1979, everybody began to take notice to what was happening at FSU.

But what is the backbone of his success?

This constantly puzzled me until I stumbled upon the chief ingredient in Bowden's *Winning Cookbook to Success*—"It's awful easy to put the blame on your staff or one of the players, but I'm the head coach, I'm responsible. If we get an intercepted pass, I threw it—I'm the head coach. If we get a punt blocked—I caused it. A bad practice, a bad game—it's up to me to assume the responsibility—I'm the head coach."

BOWDEN'S PLAN is of great design; yet, he lives mostly day-to-day doing the things he thinks should be done. When opportunity comes, he is always ready and chooses the opportunity that comes, using whatever weapons are available. His chief asset, though, is his ability to think quicker and move faster than his competition. Had Bobby Bowden been consistently wrong, then his football team would have been in much trouble. But Bowden is amazingly right—and his *success*, and *enthusiasm* and his *will to win* has brought FSU football to its proper destiny among the elite in collegiate football powers.

He might have been outstanding in any of the fields in which he is gifted—as a salesman, orator, diplomat, fighter, or executive. Bowden knows the surest paths to the hearts of men. His football, reflecting the man, is a skillful blend of science and the liveliest of arts that reflect the Grecian ideal of the sound mind in the sound body.

Bowden became a coach because it was his heart's desire, the greatest of boyhood dreams. But much of that desire dates back to a difficult day long ago when Bobby Bowden for nearly 9 months lay in bed, stricken at age 13 with rheumatic fever. Young Bobby made a convenant then with God that, if he pulled through, he would want to commit his life to serving Him in the field of athletics. Since that time, he has dignified all sports by proving that football can demand and absorb to the fullest just about every mental, emotional, and physical resource a human possesses. As a coach, he is a teaching perfectionist, a practicing psychologist, a brilliant actor, and an intellectual competitor who functions best in the white heat of urgency.

Bowden searches for the key to victory.

Bowden is always coaching, teaching, and preaching. Wit is his stage prop. I doubt if any life was ever more brilliantly organized or controlled. Even when he seems to disintegrate into emotion, he knows where he is going, how far to go. I honestly believe he allows himself to explode at times because his instinct tells him that he will get better results that way.

However, what really impresses me about Bobby Bowden is the value of his perseverance. He pursues his players with a *ruthless energy* that gets results. That one sentence reveals the *master*; a good sized cat escapes from his coaching bag. *Energy* is what a coach must have; he must pursue his men until they think as he thinks. With Bobby Bowden, it is psychological tricks—his occasional verbal roughing up, the always voluntary repairs for such damage—and for the common goal, his boys forgive and end up loving and respecting him more.

Bowden is what the psychoanalysts might call "a football complex," a bundle of instincts and conscious states, governed by the predominant idea of turning out *quality* young men and building *winning* football teams. He lives and thinks football in terms of everyday life and applies even the smallest lesson of his experience to his football theory. He knows psychology and uses it in his theory and practice. He has a healthy interest in a great number of subjects not concerned with athletics, but he extracts from these extensive pursuits, *gems* of human action and tendency, and then applies them to a football theory.

For Bowden is blessed with a natural drive and dynamic personality that is ideally adapted to handling a squad of athletes. BOWDEN IS BOSS ON THE FIELD. There is no doubt of that—and his men recognize that he utilizes his authority always with one objective: their own perfection and the superiority of the team.

Football is a game of emotion and what Coach Bowden excels at is motivation—the ways he makes believers of both his players and assistants. He tells them what the other team will try to do, and then he tells them what they'll have to do

"Now, Coach, I think we should do it this way."

to win, and invariably he is right. He makes them believe that all they have to do is follow his game plan on how to get ready for a game and then they'll win.

According to Wally Woodham, one of his starting quarterbacks, "I just knew that we were going to win nearly every game we played. Even if behind by two touchdowns in the fourth quarter, I always believed that somehow we were going to pull it out. I never knew how or when—but I did know that sooner or later we would get the much needed break—an interception, a fumble, or something. And the more important it became for FSU to win, the more certain I was that we could win."

Yes, Coach Bobby Bowden is a singular and interesting man. The years of obscurity, the many disappointments, and the long hard struggle to the top of college football is a part of Bowden that will remain forevermore. But it has given him a humility which is real and will not go away. It built a fire in him, too. Bowden blazes. Failure is abhorrent. He must be first.

And his chief coaching talent might be the ability to build the same kind of fire in the men who work for him and play the game, that Earl H. "Red" Blaik, the former great Army coach, called "closest to war."

Granted, while it may be somewhat difficult to measure the greatness of Bowden the man—even though his victories on the gridiron are recited by a massive legion of believers—those around will all agree that, if half the world had played for Coach Bobby Bowden, we'd all live in a better place.

2

Football – My Blood

*Gently the years rolled back and the book
of time opened to page one, the beginning
of the Bobby Bowden story. For much like
the narrow winding yellow brick road
which Dorothy and Toto traveled to reach
the land of Oz, or the pot of gold guarded
by Lepricons waiting at the end of the rain-
bow, everything successful must have a
proper beginning point; that special down-
home place where the road to success begins. And for Robert Cleckler Bowden that
heart-warming story began in his own hometown of Birmingham, Alabama, the undis-
puted football capital of the South . . .*

"Little did I know back then, while I was growing-up in
that white frame house behind the Woodlawn football
stadium, that someday I would become a head coach at a
major university like Florida State.

"But I did. And to me, that has to be a great example of
what young people all over this country are striving for—to
reach the American Dream.

"But like I said earlier, I did get my start in Birmingham,
Alabama, in an area of town called Woodlawn. And at the
time that they had decided to have me, my folks were living
in a small 3-bedroom white frame house, not far from the
shadows of the east endzone goalposts of Woodlawn High.

Woodlawn's stellar half-back, Bobby Bowden, was the third in a line of great passers behind Travis Tidwell and Harry Gilmer.

"When I was a boy, my Dad used to carry me up on top of the roof where we used to sit for hours upon hours watching the Woodlawn team practice. And when they were passing and punting, running plays and such, I really became infatuated with what I was seeing out on that playing field. I didn't have the foggiest idea of what was going on, but, gee whiz, it sure looked exciting. For there was something about those rich sounds I kept hearing each afternoon—the thump of shoulder pads crashing together, the bark of the head coach, and the blare of the *Colonel's* fight song being pounded out by the marching band. I could hardly wait to be a part of it all.

"And probably one of the biggest thrills that I had was when they used to practice kicking field goals. Their kicker was always pretty good and the ball used to always go sailing over the goal, across the fence and over by our chicken coop. Needless to say, it got a bit exciting for those chickens.

"But we ended up moving when I was nearly five to the East Lake section of Birmingham near the campus of Howard College (now Samford University) and there the dreams that only young boys can dream were brought to life. This time our house overlooked Berry Field, home of the Howard Bulldogs.

"Each morning as I journied to Barrett Grammar School I'd have to walk across the college campus and I'd dream of myself playing in a big Rose Bowl game like my team, the Alabama Crimson Tide, was frequently doing in those days . . . Guys like Dixie Howell, Don Hutson and Harry Gilmer, they all became my *heroes.*

"Then one day my Dad bought me a football uniform and a helmet with *Howard College Bulldogs* inscribed on it, which turned out to be a pretty big deal. And as soon as I was big enough to begin throwing and catching I'd drag my Dad out to play a game of pitch and catch, all the time thinking I could imitate the great passers at Woodlawn, Howard, or Alabama.

"*Football* sorta became ingrained into my lifestyle while I was growing up next to those football fields. I just couldn't wait to go out and play football. Everyday I'd go out early and catch passes before all of the college players got there. And if someone wanted to throw the ball, I'd go out and play catch with 'em.

"Then on Friday night, each week, Dad would take me downtown to Legion Field to see Woodlawn play teams like West End or Phillips. And by the age of 13 there was nothing I wanted more than to play for Woodlawn—it just meant too much.

"But all of the laughter and all of the dreams died in sorrow on a January afternoon that year of 1943. YMCA basketball practice had just finished that day and I could hardly make it home. My knees were killing me.

"I finally got home, though, but by the time I made that last step-up to the front porch, I just couldn't stand up on my feet, they were swollen so much.

"Mother got worried. She just couldn't understand what was happening. But after awhile, she got someone to put me in the car and quickly we raced to the doctor's office where I was examined.

"It seemed like the examination was gonna last forever. I must've aged ten years that day. And the longer it took, the greater the prospect of doom.

"When the doctor finally got through, the results were difficult to take—Rheumatic Fever—one of those diseases not yet cured by 20th century modern medicine.

"He ordered me to bed, too. Flat on my back. No sitting up. No going to the bathroom. Nothing.

"The doctor was afraid that the fever would damage my heart. And Mother cried all of the way back home. We were plenty scared.

"It was a tough time, too. America was at war. Baseball spring training in Florida was cancelled and guys like Bob Feller, Ted Williams and Joe DiMaggio were wearing khakis and fatigues instead of pinstripes and stretch socks. College football was also at a low ebb. Seventeen-year-old freshmen and 4-F's were all that was left to play on autumn Saturdays.

Bowden and high school teammate, Freddie Mims. Later, both of them went on to Alabama.

Even Joe Louis joined up with Uncle Sam to fight the *biggest bout.*

"So I laid up-there in the bed each day listening to the radio and reading books. And at 3 o'clock the doctor made his daily trek to the house to draw some blood outa my arms. Each day that needle seemed like it was getting bigger and bigger.

"But we kept at it, my family, the doctor and I. And we kept praying, too. Nearly every day the preacher came to see me. People down at Ruhama Baptist Church, or the ladies at a prayer meeting, they'd all pray for little Bobby up on 5th Avenue who's got Rheumatic Fever.

"Then one day while Mother was in my room helping me eat supper, a mighty big thing happened. Kinda like a big play in a football game when your defensive back intercepts a pass and the momentum turns to your favor.

"Mother asked me, 'Bobby, do you believe in God and that he can answer prayer if asked upon?'

"I said, 'Yes, I believe in God'—because my parents had raised me right, reading the scriptures, praying together, and being close.

"She said, 'Well, why don't you ask Him to make you well. Pray for a miracle!'

"Already I'd been praying to God about my sickness, but this time I prayed a special prayer. I said, 'Dear God, I know that I may not be worthy of a miracle but if you could heal me, or at least make me better, maybe even play again, then I'll use my life through athletics to serve You.'

"Heck, I didn't even know that I'd be able to play athletics again, but I believed. I prayed for that miracle.

"At night, the pain remained and it got worse, too. I can still remember crying myself to sleep at night because the pain was that bad.

"But slowly, bit by bit, I got to feeling better. The doctor even allowed me to sit up in bed. That's when I started making my scrapbook—cutting out new articles on the Alabama Crimson Tide and Auburn, my two closest universities, the great players and occasionally a baseball game, or two.

"That scrapbook was my only out, my only *contact* with the game I loved so much, and yearned so much to return to.

"Then one day, Dad brought home a football game on a game board for me to play. It was one of those games where it's all strategy, calling the proper plays, and matching wits with your opponent.

"One day I listened to an Alabama game on the radio when they were playing Mississippi State. According to my little game, using the same plays, Alabama should have won, but they didn't.

"However, by the end of the season Alabama had gotten much better. So did I."

3

The Miracle

The thing within Bowden, the JEV VID UD of Knute Rockne—a Norwegian expression meaning "I will will out"—must be the constantly agitating, growling, prowling. The spark within that says, "Yes, I can." This explains Bowden's intensity.

There is another ingredient in Bowden's *Winning Cookbook of Success*. The one that explains his self-motivation. That unique quality that has brought him from near tragedy at age 13, through difficult beginnings as a young coach and up to the level of success in which he has finally arrived. Such characteristics are best described in one of Bowden's favorite poems, *Don't Quit*.

When things go wrong as they sometimes will,
When the road you're trudging seems all up hill,
When the funds are low and the debts are high
And you want to smile, but you have to sigh,
When woe is pressing you down a bit,
Rest, if you must, but don't you quit.

Life is queer with its twists and turns,
As everyone of us sometimes learns,
And many a failure turns about
When he might have won had he stuck it out;
Don't give up though the pace seems slow
You may succeed with another blow.

Success is failure turned inside out
The silver tint of clouds of doubt
And you never can tell how close you are,
It may be near when it seems so far,
So stick to the fight when you're hardest hit
It's when things seem worst that you must not quit.

"When I was laid-up, all sick in bed, it could have been easy to *quit* or give-up the fight. But the word *quit* was never in my vocabulary. That was just not an alternative.

"I was always a competitor while growing up, and staying in bed and following doctor's orders required a major *sacrifice.*

"The doctor had earlier told me that I would never play football again. In addition, I was losing weight and couldn't be with boyhood pals. I was missing a lot of school time due to my sickness. And probably the biggest sacrifice I faced during the bothersome bout with Rhuematic Fever was that I was unable to get on my knees at night and pray.

"But that was part of the *challenge.* I just had to suck up my guts and face this sickness like it was an opponent on that football game that my Dad had bought me. And in order to win, I just needed to outwork that opponent.

"Probably one of the most amazing blessings that I received was that I always had lots of people coming by to cheer me up. They'd always say, "Come on Bobby, don't give-up, you can beat this thing."

"These were great words of encouragement, and the more and more that I heard them, I just couldn't help but believe that I'd come back and get well. Mother and Dad preached this to me day and night. I just never quit believing them.

"Gradually, I was able to get out of the bed and move about the house. Then later the doctor let me walk around for short periods of time. But he had one more order, too: NO PHYSICAL EXERCISE.

"And for a youngster who lived and died with Alabama football, this was awful tough to take. My biggest goal in life at age 13 was to one day play for Coach Frank Thomas at

During the off-season, Bobby Bowden played in the Lee Jordan Band while at Woodlawn.

Alabama and maybe have the opportunity to play in a Rose Bowl game. Yet, with this illness, it just didn't seem like I'd ever get there. But I knew God had a plan for my life and if I was supposed to play football again—it would happen.

"So after making up my eighth grade year at Barrett Grammar School I finally was able to walk-in the front doors of Woodlawn High. Boy, it was a big place!

"I was just a little guy, too. About 5'5" and 120 lbs. And with Dr. Mahafey still opposed to football there was little for me to do except go to school.

"But when I got there that first day and saw the varsity practicing in Woodlawn Stadium, I just knew that I had to do something to be a part of the school program.

"Football and all other sports had been ruled out of the picture. And I knew the Doc wouldn't go along with me being a student manager; the only prospect remaining was the band.

"Now, I had been playing the piano since I was eight and had played a bit of trumpet in grammar school, too, so learning another musical instrument was only a matter of want-to and hard work.

"So I joined the band that year. There were too many trumpet players, though. Instead, they made me a trombone man. And not long afterwards I was marching in a gold and white uniform on Friday nighs at Legion Field.

"It made me feel good to be out there, kinda like I was contributing something to the school. After all, I was a small part of the football team.

"Then by my sophomore year I was lucky enough to make the school orchestra, which was a big deal.

"By then, some of us got to thinking we were pretty good and formed a jazz combo called the Lee Jordan band. On weekends we played at the old *Rose Club*, an after-dinner dance club in east Birmingham near Irondale. And it was amazing how well the old folks warmed up to us, leaving tips and patting us on the back. It was really a thrill.

"On Wednesdays, we'd play at the weekly school dances down at the *Colonel's Corner*, just a few blocks from

"I always was a ham for photos."

Woodlawn High. The music was strictly bebop and everyone danced the jitterbug. Our theme song was the popular hit, *Deep Purple.*

"Mother and Dad never could figure out what a bunch of us teenagers used to do down there. All of the girls would dress in long skirts and bobby socks. And the boys looked like something out of *Happy Days* wearing blue jeans, white T-shirts, crew cuts, with an occasional starched shirt and bow tie mixed in for a change in pace.

The thing within Bowden, the JEV VIL UD of Knute Rockne—a Norwegian expression meaning "I will will out"—must be the constantly agitating, growling, prowling. The spark within that says, "Yes, I can." This explains Bowden's intensity.

"I still yearned to step back out on the gridiron and play the game I loved so much. But the thing that held me back was the doctor. He still wouldn't let me play.

"Time and time again, Mother and I kept going back to see him, each time the doctor had the same diagnosis.

"He said, 'I'm sorry Bobby, you won't ever play football again. Your sports are over. I don't want you running, lifting weights, nothing; I don't want you doing anything that will push your heart.'

"Then he added the clincher. 'If you do any of these, then your heart won't be able to take it. It will give out by the time you're 38.'

"Now this scared my parents and me. We just didn't understand. My health had been really good. And besides, there had been no problem since that first accident. We just couldn't live with that decision. There had to be a second opinion.

"Finally, Mother took me to a heart specialist, Dr. George Warwick. This time we had to find out what my status was: football or no football.

"Well, he examined me and I really didn't think I had a chance. Supposedly there was scar tissue built-up around my heart, and physical exercise would only make things worse. But when he got through there was good news.

"Dr. Warwick said, 'Bobby, your heart is as good as anybody's. The scar tissue has all healed. Go get 'em! Sic 'em!'

"I remember breaking down and crying that day, right in the same room with Mother and Dr. Warwick. I just couldn't help it, for it seemed as if a tremendous burden had been lifted. No doubt about it, I was definitely the luckiest guy around. God had really blessed me.

"So I went out for fall training that year, although like most youngsters that age, I was small in stature. Actually I was just a runt. But I went at 'em full speed because I had something to prove. I knew that I belonged.

"Things were going well, too. Coach Kenny Morgan, who was one of the best coaches in Alabama, made me a tailback in the old Notre Dame Box system which required a lot of blocking. And I turned out to be a fairly good blocker, being able to get lower than most guys.

"However, two weeks before the first game an accident occurred while I was running out for a pass. Unfortunately, my right thumb was broken and Coach Morgan attempted to reset it and secure the thumb with tape. But that didn't work. As a matter of fact, I have a suspicion that Coach Morgan helped complete the fracture.

"Dr. Sherrill, the orthopedic surgeon who took care of the great Alabama teams, later reset the broken thumb and placed it in a cast. Needless to say, my hope to play football that fall appeared quite bleak.

"Coach Morgan had a plan, though. He called me at home and said, "Well, I'd like to redshirt you this year. If your parents will let you lay out of school, that'll give you two more years of eligibility at Woodlawn."

"I talked it over with Mother and Dad and they agreed, thus allowing me to sit out of school that fall and preserving an extra year of eligibility.

"And when school started in January, 1947, once again I was part of the team, playing behind David Booker and Billy Gilmer (Harry Gilmer's brother) at tailback in spring training. However, when we lined up in the fall, I was able to work my way up and eventually become a starter.

Woodlawn quarterback, Bobby Bowden, and young friend before 1948 Crippled Children's Game.

"I've gotta admit it was a long road back. But thank God that I did make it."

Yes, young Bobby Bowden had amassed the much needed vitality for the game he wanted so badly to play. He eventually became a quarterback—a *star* All-State quarterback. And when it came time to pick a school to play for, Alabama came courting. Yes, they wanted him.

And when it was over, Bobby achieved his dream of a lifetime. He signed his scholarship with his beloved Alabama team.

4

The American Dream

Only in the Bobby Bowden dream-come-true fairy-tale would a youngster give-up a football scholarship at the college for which he had longed a life-time to play, instead to run away and secretly marry his high school sweetheart and together to go on to a small Baptist college and find big time success—he as a Little All-American, she as a football cheerleader and mother of three.

"Ever since those days when Dad used to drag me up on top of the roof to watch those great Woodlawn High teams play, football has always held a special place in my life. It was just part of my up-bringing.

"When I was just a youngster, the game was reaching its golden age. Collegiate football boasted colorful characters, great excitement, tremendous school spirit and a brand of play that few were ever again to witness. The great rivalries—Alabama-Tennessee, Army-Navy, Notre Dame-USC, Georgia-Georgia Tech, Michigan-Ohio State—yes, these were the powerhouses that ruled America's game.

"There were many an autumn Saturday afternoon when I would sit there by my radio listening to those great rivals play their gridiron game. And so often, especially during my sickness, I would find myself dreaming of playing in those great games, perhaps being the guy making a long run, throwing a terrific pass, or making the unbelievable catch.

"Guys like Don Hutson, Harry Gilmer, Johnny Lujack, Creighton Miller, Doc Blanchard, Glenn Davis or Tom Harmon, these were my heroes of the late 1930's and early 40's.

"Also, some of America's greatest coaches were barking their commands from the sidelines during this eventful period. It was almost a Who's Who List of College Coaches: Frank Leahy, Elmer Layden, Jim Crowley, Red Blaik, Frank Thomas, Dana X. Bible, Paul Brown, Pop Warner and General Bob Neyland.

"So often while I was laid up in bed, flat on my back, I questioned myself and my God—would I be able to come-back? Would I ever be able to play again the game I loved so much?

"And the more I asked these questions, the more I dreamed of coming back and playing football. Creighton Miller was no longer just a Notre Dame running back scampering for 40 yards and the winning touchdown against Ohio State—I, in a sense, became Creighton Miller. His touchdown was my touchdown. And when Frank Leahy called Johnny Lujack to the sidelines to discuss a critical play to be used against Michigan—I stood in Lujack's shoes. Leahy was discussing the play with me.

"And with each new Saturday there was a new adventure, a new game. It might be a great Alabama team playing against a very tough USC squad, and Harry Gilmer was running and passing behind the great blocking of Holt Rast and Vaughn Mancha, all the time leading them on the way to another Rose Bowl victory. On those days, I was Gilmer.

"Yet, some days I dreamed of the classic game, Notre Dame vs. Army, Frank Leahy vs. Red Blaik; Lujack, Leon Hart and big George Conners vs. Blanchard and Davis and the West Point gang. Sadly, it was a game that never took place. World War II took care of that.

"But each afternoon that the immortal dream game was to be played I always chose to play for Notre Dame. Perhaps it was because of the great Notre Dame winning tradition or maybe it was because in real life, Blanchard and Davis actually led their great Army team to successive wins over a

Howard College during 1951 game at Berry Field.

Notre Dame squad lacking the greatness of a Lujack or a Leon Hart in 1944 and 1945.

"No matter the reason, though, I wanted the Fighting Irish to win. I wanted Frank Leahy to inspire me to victory just like he had inspired guys like Ziggy Czarobski, Jim Martin and Emil "Red" Sitko to go out and win another game in the name of their blessed school, Notre Dame.

"Somehow these emotion filled games seemed so life-like, for they were always played in big stadiums, packed with sell-out crowds. And with each big play, each daring moment, there was always excitement or silence, enthusiasm or despair.

"Finally, when each memorable dream was over, much like a book just read, it was carefully stored away on a specially reserved bookshelf somewhere in the back of my mind awaiting another day, another game to be played."

Oh, how great it would have been to have lived and played in that wonderful world of yesterday. When ticket-tape parades for time-honored heroes were the order of the day. And when big brassy bands played the Star-Spangled Banner and Americans actually sang the words.

But America has changed and it now seems that in this country of ours, Americans are caught up in a short supply of national leaders to look up to, briskly and enthusiastically created giants—athletic giants—with whom they are more willing to identify.

For it is into this milieu of mixed-up passions and exalted public imagery that the name Bobby Bowden is projected.

For like the stories of Frank Merriwell, Horatio Alger, Babe Ruth, Abe Lincoln, or Jack the Giant Killer, the story of FSU's Bobby Bowden is one winning tale destined for immortality.

For there is special magic in this man, and a kindred magic in his name. Inevitably, certain questions are posed. Has Bobby Bowden become a living legend because of the checkered trappings of the fabled 1970's? Is Bowden a product of his times or has he helped make the times?

The questions are legitimate but not easily answered. Yet

Little All-America, Bobby Bowden, at Howard College.

1951 all

1. DeVan Robbins, End, Utah State.
2. Bobby Bowden, Back, Howard College.
3. Jack Cross, Back, Utah.
4. Andy Davis, Back, George Washington.
5. Charley Maze, Guard, Howard College.
6. Tom Scott, End, Virginia.

TKA Team

7. Jimmy Lesane, Back, Virginia.
8. Ray Archangeletti, Guard, Miami, Fla.
9. Bob Davis, Center, Tennessee.
10. Dick Patrick, Tackle, Oregon.
11. Walter Fisher, Tackle, Rutgers.

the consensus would be that Bowden is not just a synthetic hero manufactured in the Hollywood process which gives America dozens of notorious, star-crossed celebrities; for Bowden is self-made, self-starting and self-propelled. He needs no publicity build-up, no false coloration, no trumpeting of nonexistant values.

And in this fast whirling society where winning is the only thing people are interested in—whether it's beating the stock market, the elements, Uncle Sam, or even rising above one's origins and the prejudices of others—Bobby Bowden as a man stands tall. He is the perfect example, America's archetype of a winner.

Wherever he goes these days there is always one important fact of life—the presence of Robert Cleckler Bowden dominates everything and everyone, whether on the football field, at a coaches meeting, a social function, or a business meeting. And if there is one element of his personality that is preeminent, it is his flair for leadership. Bowden was born to lead.

Sing your praises of the Johnny Majors', the Joe Paterno's, the U.S.C.'s, and the Alabama's, but down in Tallahassee, Florida, Bobby Bowden has taken a once all-female college and set off *something* that is national in significance.

For Bowden has *developed* a new philosophy and a new way of life in the deep South—the kind that yields quality young men and winning football teams—the kind that the noted columnist of the 1920's, Westbrook Pegler described best.

He called it *believing.*

5

The Big Surprise

All of the thrills and fanfare of big time football were apparent that night in Birmingham's Legion Field as Woodlawn and arch-rival Ramsey High opened up the Big Five football season. There were banners, balloons, a crackerjack band, pretty majorettes, and a darned good football game, which Ramsey went on later to win, 13-6.

Yet, there were no words to describe the early autumn scene as the grounds keeper turned the lights out for the National Anthem to be played. A beautiful full moon shone down on the darkened stadium, reflecting a pale glow in the glimmering eyes of the on-looking crowd. Slowly, the color guard raised the spotlighted flag and the Woodlawn band played the "Star Spangled Banner" while 22,000 proud Americans sang.

To young Bobby Bowden, co-captain of the Woodlawn squad, this would be the biggest game of his life, truly a night that he would remember for a long, long time.

However, there were two other very memorable adventures for young Bowden during the 1940's.

"Vaughn Mancha is one of those great football players you always remember. Even my scrapbook that I kept as a youngster was filled with pages of photos and press clippings

"That's one place I never wanted to go."

of Vaughn Mancha, an All-America center for the Crimson Tide.

"He was impressive, too, kinda like the Rock of Gibraltar. Vaughn stood 6'2", and weighed 245-lbs., which was unheard of in those World War II days of 190-lb. tackles. And each week before an opposing nose-guard had the privilege of facing him on the field, Vaughn would always send him a letter of instruction: *Dear Spamo, Just so you won't end up hungry on Saturday I'm advising you to bring along an extra apple for a snack 'cause I'm going to eat your lunch. Kindest regards, Vaughn.*

"Now off the field, most football players usually appear smaller in stature than when prepared for gridiron combat. But not big Vaughn Mancha. He looked just awsome.

"Once, while attending Col. Butler's summer band camp at the University of Alabama in 1945, just guess who happened to be in the same lunch line together at Julia Tutwiler Hall? You're right. The big two; Vaughn Mancha and Bobby Bowden.

"Now, my day had been going really great until, suddenly, I heard from the back of the line, 'Hey, Mancha, save us some food how 'bout it.'

"It took me a few moments, but I finally mustered enough courage to turn around. And when I did, there he was, Mt. Rushmore, himself, standing there with hands on hips, just daring me to make a move.

"He asked, 'What's your name little-man?'

"Half-frightened I answered, 'Sir, aaahhh, Bobby Bowden from Woodlawn High.'

"He then asked, 'You ever heard of Harry Gilmer, he's my teammate.'

"Now, everybody had heard of the famous freshman, Harry Gilmer, who could run and throw better than any quarterback alive except for Red Grange, and who in his first year at Alabama had led his team to the Sugar Bowl where he dazzled the fans with his famous jump passes. But when big Vaughn asked if I knew Gilmer, I smarted-off, kinda like a suicide case and replied, 'Yeah, he's a Woodlawn boy.'

"Big Vaughn should have thrown me up against the wall for that one. Luckily, he just smiled. And all the time while standing there, I kept thinking to myself, 'How do I keep these scrawny hands from being crushed if this big ape who's also from Birmingham, wants to shake hands.' For some reason or another fate never allowed that to happen.

"Years later, however, when Bill Peterson hired me away from Howard to join his staff at Florida State, I ran into Vaughn again. This time we were on friendlier terms but I still had to look-up to him, Vaughn Mancha was the Athletic Director and that made him the boss and a good one, too. And until this day, I've kept looking-up to Vaughn Mancha. He was just that impressive."

*   *   *   *   *

"When I got to Alabama in the spring of '49, I had the pleasure of meeting two other guys at my position who looked awful impressive, Ed Salem and Bobby Marlow and when they stepped on the playing field they ran pretty impressive too. Salem eventually became an All-America, and Marlow would end up becoming the leading rusher in the SEC for the 1950's. Even big All-America linemen like Bob Gain at Kentucky, or Notre Dame's George Conner would have had their problems defensing those two.

"So here comes Bobby Bowden, the rookie, who happens to be playing the same position. I must have been real confident or pretty dumb to have considered those kind of odds. But I was never one to back off from a challenge.

"And, after a few days of Spring training, I began to feel good about what I was trying to accomplish on the field running and passing and returning punts—the kind of things that I used to do at Woodlawn.

"Unfortunately, that Spring of 1949 I had a severe case of homesickness. I really missed my mother and dad. I especially missed Ann, my high school sweetheart, who still had one semester remaining at Woodlawn before her graduation.

"During the off-season at Howard, I ran track."

"No doubt about it, Ann Estock was a looker. She had moved into Birmingham during her sophomore year across the street from a good friend of mine, Mort Vasserberg. Soon afterwards every boy in school was sitting on her doorstep including yours truly. Needless to say, I started visiting Mort's house a lot.

"Ann was just about everything a girl could be in those days: beauty queen, cheerleader, the sweetheart of one thing or another. You name it, she did it. Plus, she was the best-looking gal you or I have ever laid eyes on. So you can see, I was pretty lucky to have her committed to me, or at least I thought committed to me.

"It seems that the summer before my senior year at Wood-lawn, Ann had met a good friend of mine, 'Shorty' White who played running back at neighboring Phillips High. Shorty and I had been in Panama City, Florida, together that summer and she evidently had heard about our week-in-the-sun escapades from him.

"Now, Ann was the type that didn't like any female competition messing around her territory. And when Ol' Bobby headed off to Alabama in January, she decided to teach me a lesson as a reminder of my previous mischievous doings in Panama City that summer. Luckily, I found out about her plot through my roommate, Paul Crumbley, who was also from Birmingham.

"Paul had gone home that weekend and when he returned on that cold, February Sunday afternoon, he came up to the room and said, 'Bobby, aren't you and Ann still going steady?'

"And I said, 'Yeah.'

"Well, ol' Paul looked at me real funny and with his hands on his hips and jaw half-twisted, he said, 'Are you sure?'

"I said, 'Yeah.' But the way Paul looked, I knew something just had to be up.

"Finally, Paul broke down and told me the story of how he had seen Ann and Shorty riding on the East Lake streetcar together on the way back from the movies in town. To Paul something just had to be wrong.

"and played baseball, too."

"I was really horrible
in basketball."

"There was. Plenty.

"And when I got on the phone that night both Ann and I did a lot of soul-searching. Things just had to resolved, real soon.

"Well, I went home after practice that next weekend and ol' Bobby really did some slick sweet-talking. As a matter of fact, Ann and I started talking about how great it would be to get married. She wanted a little white house with a picket fence. I just wanted to say, "I do."

Our folks, however, thought that was pure rubbish. After all, I was only 19 and Ann was still sweet 16. They had plans for us both to attend college, get an education, and hopefully become *somebody.* But we were too headstrong and too much in love. There just couldn't be anything better than getting married at this wonderful moment in our lives.

"It went on like that for about a month. Everytime we tried to discuss marriage, our folks would want to change the subject and discuss the news, or something.

"Well, Ann and I were determined to get married, one way or another. So we started planning, snooping around and asking a lot of questions. Quickly we found out that a lot of kids our age at school had also been bitten with the Spring love bug and had decided to elope by driving across the state line to Georgia to get married.

"That was great news. The only problem was trying to find an opportunity that would permit us to be gone long enough to ride over to Rising Fawn, Georgia and say, "We do."

"So I began thinking about the situation at hand and attempted to put it into a football perspective, trying to think, 'Now what would Leahy or Rockne do in this situation.' And that's when I realized that eloping was a lot like throwing a 60-yard bomb to your split end. The fundamental key in both instances was *timing.*

"Finally, on the first weekend of April, opportunity struck as both of our parents just happened to be out of town visiting relatives. Somehow I knew Lady Luck had to be involved in all of this because when I got home from school,

Dad's car was sitting in the driveway looking spiffy and polished like it had nothing to do all weekend.

"Hurriedly, I ran into the house, got some money that I had been saving, rushed back out of the house, jumped in the car, and then drove to Ann's hoping all of the time that she hadn't decided to spend the night at a girlfriend's house.

"But when I got there she was at home. And once again, I had this warm feeling inside that somebody upstairs was watching out for Ol' Bobby.

"So we packed a lunch bag and drove to Rising Fawn, Georgia. The entire trip Ann and I kept asking each other whether, or not, the Justice-of-the-Peace would marry us once we got there.

"It took about four hours and one tank of gas to drive over there. The justice of the peace only took 10 minutes and a $20 bill, and when we walked out of his office, both Ann and I stopped on the sidewalk, looked at each other— she winked and I smiled, then we both burst out laughing. Later, Ann asked, 'Bobby, what have you got us into?'

"I replied, 'A lot of trouble.'

"So on the return trip to Birmingham, Ann and I promised to keep our marriage a secret until we could figure out a way to break the news real gently to our parents.

"But like all women, Ann couldn't keep a secret and within a week the entire Woodlawn cheerleading squad had heard the news. I knew then it was time to face Mother, Dad and the Estocks.

"Boy, were they ever surprised."

6

Humble Beginnings

Knowing that things would probably never get much better at Howard unless a commitment was made to big-time winning, Bowden placed that once-in-a-lifetime phone call and took the South Georgia job, sight unseen.

The day Bobby Bowden, the small but scrappy All-American, graduated from Howard College in January of 1953, he quickly pushed aside any notions about becoming a professional football player and competing against the great players of the time like Kyle Rote, Charlie Conerly, or Bobby Layne. To Bowden only one brand really excited him—college football. He wanted to be a college coach.

When Earl Gartman, head coach at Howard, told young Bowden, "Get your master's and we'll hire you," the feisty young man wasted no time. He commuted back and forth every week from Birmingham to Nashville for seven months in order to obtain a master's degree in physical education from George Peabody College (now a division of Vanderbilt University).

And in the fall of 1953, when college football programs began to gear their teams up for the difficult task of another season, young Bowden was returning from Nashville with his diploma in hand and an invitation from Dr. Davis, the president of Howard College to become an assistant at his beloved alma mater. Yes, things were looking good for Bobby Bowden.

Upon his arrival, however, he and Dr. Davis had a slight misunderstanding in regards to his salary. It seems that Dr. Davis had this hard-line belief that first year assistants should receive only $3,300 a year for their work. But Bowden, in the meantime, kept contending that Davis had promised him $3,600 only seven months beforehand. To young Bowden, a promise given meant a promise kept.

Being president of a Baptist college, as well as a football fan who wanted a winning team to cheer for, Dr. Davis agreed on the additional $300 in salary for young Bowden in hopes that it might encourage the new assistant to put some sparkle into an already losing program.

Things were tough for the low-budgeted program at Howard. There were no scholarships and only a few meager jobs for athletes, such as sweeping the gym floor or loading coal into the school furnace.

Yet, when the school administrators began to search to fill the head coaching position that Earl Gartman had vacated when he became the Athletic Director, there was only one man they wanted—an established coach, Cannonball White, who had previously coached Howard to many glorious days before World War II. Cannonball, at the time, was a 62-year old head coach at the University of Sewanee, where he had also built another winning program. But when Birmingham called, Cannonball listened, and soon was coaching the Howard Bulldogs once again.

In the two years that followed, eager-to-learn Bobby Bowden began to grasp a lot of football philosophy from the other two members of the Howard coaching staff. As it turned out, Bowden took charge of the backs and receivers, while Cannonball schooled the remainder of the offense and left the defensive chores to Gartman, who still insisted on working with the team. After two years, the team had posted only three victories, and an aging Cannonball White decided to retire. Gartman resigned, later to become the head coach of Austin Peay. With only Bowden left from the staff, Howard College was once again faced with the unpleasant dilemma of finding a new head coach.

Bowden thought himself a shoo-in for the job but Howard administrators considered him much too young for the responsibilities that the position carried.

Feeling disheartened, Bowden went home one afternoon only to find a letter awaiting him. It read:

IF YOU WANT TO BE HEAD COACH AT SOUTH GEORGIA PHONE ME COLLECT. DR. WILLIAM SMITH, PRESIDENT.

Knowing that things would probably never get much better at Howard unless a commitment was made to big-time winning, Bowden placed that once-in-a-lifetime phone call and took the South Georgia job, sight unseen.

When he arrived at Douglas, Bowden quickly discovered that little South Georgia was certainly not a step-up from Howard. Here was a two-year college in a town of less than 10,000—some difference from Birmingham. But the 24 year-old coach was determined to make his program work. And he set out with one goal in mind—to change the football futures in this sleepy paced town.

At the time, South Georgia offered only 18 scholarships, all of them partial. And none of them were earmarked for just football. They even varied in their amounts—six were for $120, six for $90 and the remaining six were for $60. Considering an annual tuition cost of $200, Bowden knew that some changes would have to be made.

So he set out that first summer going from store to store, calling upon the local merchants asking, "Would you please donate money for our football program:" And when it was over, the energetic new coach had raised nearly $3,000 to aid his major reconstruction program.

Then, when fall football started and little South Georgia had tucked two impressive victories under its belt, the youthful coach learned one of the first lessons that all new coaches always end up learning the hard way.

"It was in the third ballgame," Bowden was later to admit, "and we were undefeated and playing Jones Junior College over in Mississippi, who later that year would play in the Junior College Rose Bowl in Pasadena, California.

"Anyway, we had already won two games and I got the bighead by thinking that I was the long-awaited answer to the coaching profession and that I'd probably win every game, hands down.

"Unfortunately, I got humbled real quick-like as we got beat something awful, 61-14. We were just plain lucky to get out of that game alive."

Bowden then added, "Going home after the game, I took it real hard, knowing that I had the responsibility of the team and then seeing them get beat that bad. It was the first time that quitting actually ever crossed my mind. I had just never had the responsibility before, or the pain of losing. Boy, for the next few days I had some doubts."

But South Georgia, the small, two-year college went head-on the next two weeks with 4-year powers Troy State and Jacksonville State, and earned a high mark of respect. Especially against Jax State which had already played seven games and had been unscored upon. That day, South Georgia scored twice in a losing cause, but went on to win the remainder of their schedule that season and the state Junior College crown.

The next year, former high school teammate, Vince Gibson, joined Bowden at South Georgia and the two of them began to learn a lot of football together—the hard way.

It all began with the transfer of an oversized Indian who had flunked out of school at Florida State. One must remember, of course, that at South Georgia the coaches hunted *everything* that could walk, so when he walked in, everybody paid attention to him. He stood 6'4", weighed 235 lbs., and was all man, the kind of football player that all coaches get impressed about—especially, when he's 28 years old.

But after 2 weeks, opinions began to change. It was 2 a.m. on morning and the phone jolted Bobby and Ann Bowden out of bed. It was the town's sheriff on the phone and he sounded upset.

He told Bowden, "Coach, I've got one of your boys down here."

"Which one?" Bowden asked.

"This Injun fella," the sheriff said. "He's just tried to burn down the jailhouse."

So very early in the morning, Bowden headed to the County Jail to get his newly acquired star pupil out of the pokey. When he arrived, the coach learned that his player had gotten into a fight at a local gas station, while drinking.

Bowden told him, "You can't do things like fighting around here. You're supposed to be a football player and an example to the community. If you want to fight then go over to the next county and fight. Just don't do things around here."

The next weekend, Bowden received another early morning call. This time it was from the sheriff in the next county. It seems the big Injun had gone over to the next county and whipped the entire deputy sheriff's squad in a barroom brawl.

Bowden and Gibson were bewildered. They tried everything—preaching to him, taking him to church and Sunday school.

Eventually, they found out that the Indian had been in jail, cut-up in a knife fight, and could only see out of one eye. Later, he straightened up and began attending church.

But things happen, and one day the big guy finally cursed a student assistant coach who had been working him real hard in practice.

As soon as Bowden saw the commotion, he called the redman over for a Knute Rockne type lecture. "I told him that hitting an assistant coach is just like hitting me and a player is not going to do those things. I asked him if he understood."

"He said, 'No!'"

"So, we ran him all afternoon when all of a sudden he comes up to me in practice and says, 'Coach, I want to be made an example. In practice tomorrow I'm going to walk up to you and I want you to draw back and hit me as hard as you can on my chin. I'm just gonna stand there and take it to show the team I'm loyal to you.'

"Now, tell me, can you believe this shot."

Mrs. GEORGIA of 58

SPONSORED BY
Savannah Gas Company
Gas Light Company of Columbus

Mrs. Savannah

"There's Ann stealing the show again, as she wins the Mrs. Georgia title."

Mrs. GEORGIA of '58

Mrs. AMERICA ★  Sponsored by

FORT LAUDERDALE. FLA. Savannah Gas Co.

MAY 5TH - 11TH Gas Light Company Of Columbus

...th Georgia

Mrs. Columbus

Mrs. North Georgia

South Georgia was a proving ground for future head coaches, Bobby Bowden and Vince Gibson.

"Our first spring training at South Georgia was one big gut check."

"Coach Bryant, Texas A&M and that war-camp at Junction never had it this good."°

"Later, Vince Gibson joined up with us and we began to mold our team."

"I knew then he had a loose screw, but we never had a problem that season until the last game when he called an assistant coach a SOB.

"So after practice I walked in the locker room and found him playing darts with Vince Gibson. He had those darts and he also had a funny look in his eye, kinda like he knew he was in trouble. And all of the time I kept thinking to myself that he's gonna throw one of those things at our heads.

"No doubt about it," Bowden added, "That fella just *had* to go.

"So I went by his domitory room that evening and told him my thoughts. I told him that if he packed his bags that evening and drove over to Southern Mississippi at Hattiesburg, Mississippi a football scholarship had already been arranged for him.

"Well, he did as I thought and left the campus that night hitching a ride to Hattiesburg. Then, two nights later I got a call at 3 a.m. from the big Injun.

"He said, 'Coach you lied to me—how come?'

"That night I couldn't sleep, and the next morning I called the sheriff and explained to him not to let that Injun back on campus. But looking back, now, I can see that I turned my back on that guy. I vowed then never to do it again."

There were other hard times, too, for Bowden. Part of his original football deal with South Georgia called upon him to be the bus driver on out of town trips and also to be the head basketball coach. But after an inaugural 1-13 basketball season, Bowden soon convinced school officials to let him concentrate his talents on football.

Housing was a problem, too. And Ann and Bobby Bowden with three youngsters, and a fourth one on the way, had to do everything possible to stretch his meager $4,500 salary. So Bowden and family solved the problem and moved into an old Air Corps barracks that had once been an Officer's Club during the war—the kind that had two large baths, heaters in every room and cement floors that sweated during the winter and required newspaper to be placed upon them to soak up the moisture.

Bowden during brief moment of relaxation at South Georgia.

Once, when his wife Ann was pregnant with her fourth child and labor pains had suddenly awakened them in the middle of the night, Bowden was confronted with an immediate crisis. But like the great strategist that he was on the field, he quickly solved the problem, brilliantly, by placing Ann in the front seat of the family station wagon and then dragging a mattress into the back where he parked three sleepy kids for the trip to the hospital.

During the summer, Bowden supplemented his income to provide for a growing family of six by working the graveyard shift from 8 p.m. until 8 a.m. as the scale man in a tobacco farm.

"It was a place called Stubbs Warehouse and I can still remember taking naps atop the piles of tobacco when work slowed at 2 or 3 in the morning, only to be awakened by enormous rats running across the fresh tobacco or, on occasions, me."

To depict how tight the economics were for Bowden at South Georgia, he once had the opportunity to hire some badly needed additonal coaching help. So he packed up the family station wagon and headed toward St. Augustine, Fla., to hire a successful high school coach. According to Bowden, "We got near St. Augustine and came upon a 50-cent toll bridge. We couldn't come up with the money, so we had to double back and avoid that bridge."

The assistant coach that he was hiring was Vince Gibson, who later became an FSU assistant with Bowden and now is head coach at Tulane.

Bowden, however, did receive a raise when their fourth toddler came. And when it did, Ann had a proper use for the money. What happened to it? Well, until today Bowden still calls it "the biggest problem our marriage has had in 31 years."

It seems that the ink was hardly dry on the first check when Ann went out and bought a piano. "Not one of those little, cheap babies—one of those big ol' grand pianos."

Bowden hit the roof when he found out, for the young coach barely had enough money to take care of the kids and

"Coach Gartman taught me how to outwork my opponents."

keep food on the table. "And here's Ann going out and blowing all of our savings. Let me tell you, those monthly payments were tough . . . Every month when that bill came in, it nearly broke up our marriage."

Today, the Bowdens still own that piano and it plays as though it was bought only yesterday. Thankfully, it was paid for long ago.

Things eventually got better at South Georgia. Bowden even got a rent-free apartment in a dormitory, Powell Hall. He and Ann were charged with the duty of acting as house parents of the dorm. But even with their duties and the four little Bowdens, Ann remained attractive as well as active, and in 1956, she was named Mrs. South Georgia.

And it was at this sleepy paced school in the rural backwoods of South Georgia that Bobby Bowden learned the biggest lesson of his young life.

It seems that the incident occurred when Bowden was sitting in their apartment in Powell Hall when he heard some firecrackers explode. Racing outside, he found only one suspect. This one happened to be a young man of questionable reputation, who had been a lot of trouble already at school.

So Bowden grabbed him and said, "You did that, didn't you."

And the boy said, "No, sir."

Convinced otherwise, Bowden took him the next day to the Dean to have him dismissed from school. But one of Bowden's players stepped forward at the last moment and told him, "Coach, it was me who did it."

After that experience, Bowden recalled, "I learned then to never accuse a young man of doing something wrong unless I see him do it. In the situation at South Georgia, I already had a prejudice against the young man in the first place and that controlled my sense of rationale—my good reasoning and my emotions. Since that day, I've tried to learn not to be prejudiced of people."

7

Disappointment

Walking to his office just two blocks away, Bowden began to reminisce of those days that he had spent as a youngster just waiting for the day when he'd be a football coach. And now, when the young and jittery gridiron genius had finally reached that goal, suddenly it was disappearing from his grasp. Things were just too difficult to understand.

In four memorable years, 1955 through 1958, at tiny South Georgia, Bobby Bowden had built a winning program which sported a 22-11 record and three Georgia State junior college championships. Winning, however, wasn't enough to satisfy the school trustees when the bills had to be paid. And after the 1958 season, President Smith called Bowden in to discuss the program's financial woes.

He said, "Bobby, we're gonna have to drop football here— we're just not making any money."

Bowden was shocked. But after a few moments, when he had gathered his thoughts, he responded. "Well, we could try to raise more support from the community. Don't you think that would work?"

Dr. Smith just nodded his head. "That would be great but we're already getting more contributions from the town than they can afford. No, we're just gonna drop the program and try to clear up the financial situation here."

Bowden just shrugged his shoulders and said, "O.K., whatever you decide," and then walked toward the door.

"1955, South Georgia. Our first State Championship."

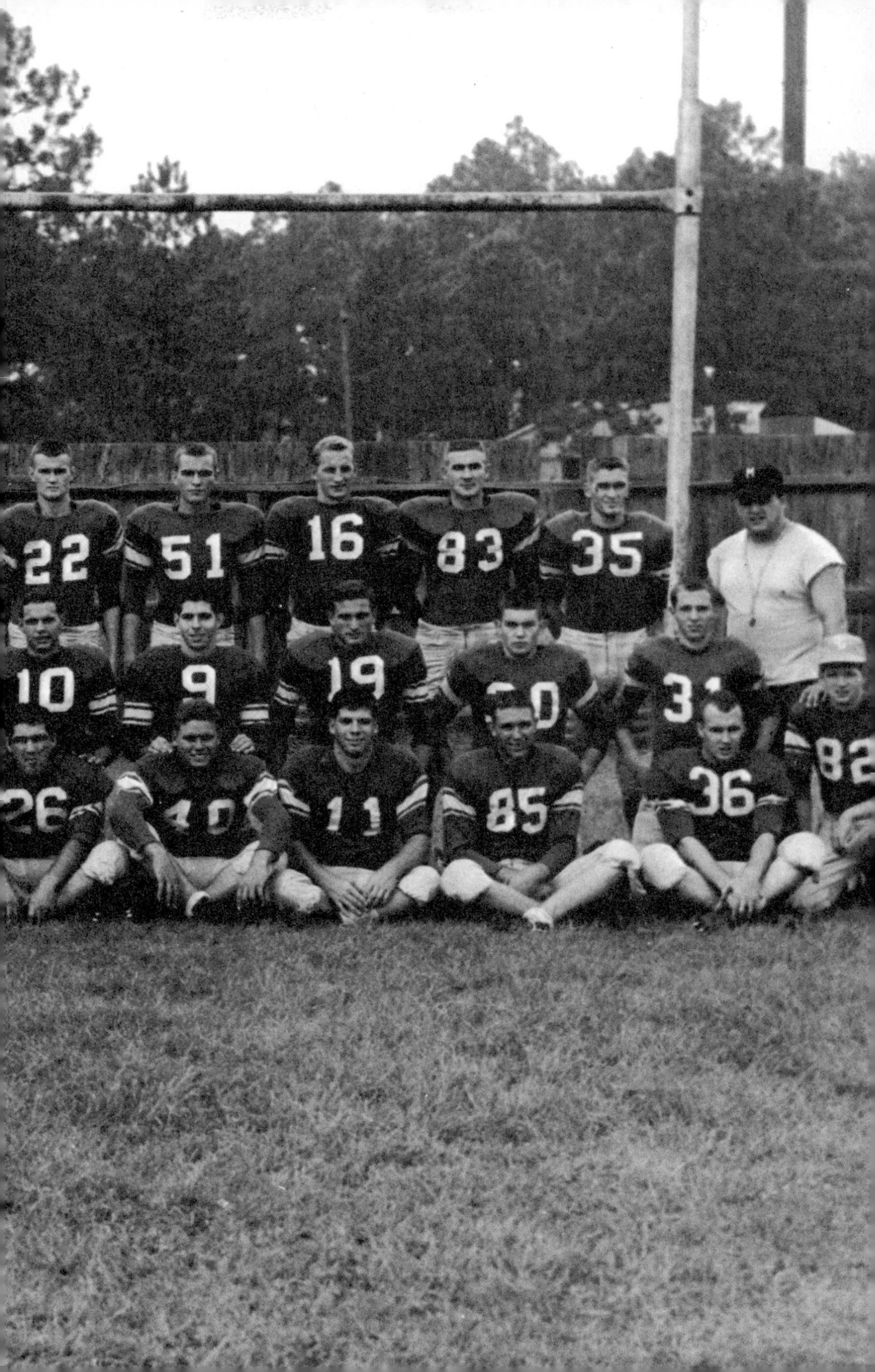

MPS — 1956 ↗

"1956, South Georgia. We got lucky and won it again."

It took a determined bunch of young men to win at South Georgia.

President Smith, however, had some comforting news for young Bowden. He said, "Bobby, we want you to stay on here as our Athletic Director and Head Baseball Coach, or whatever. We just want you to stay with us."

Walking to his office just two blocks away, Bowden began to reminisce of those days that he had spent as a youngster just waiting for the day when he'd be a football coach. And now, when the young and jittery gridiron genius had finally reached that goal, suddenly, it was disappearing from his grasp. Things were just too difficult to understand.

But in every dark cloud of despair there is always a silver lining. Four years earlier, in similar dispair, the youthful Bobby Bowden had found a letter waiting for him—an opportunity to be a head coach. Now another opportunity had come, as he walked into his office and on his desk he saw—a letter—from Dr. Leslie Wright, the new president of Howard College. He opened it and read:

DEAR COACH BOWDEN,

IF YOU ARE INTERESTED IN BECOMING THE NEW HEAD COACH AT HOWARD PLEASE LET US KNOW. KINDEST REGARDS,

DR. LESLIE WRIGHT, PRESIDENT
HOWARD COLLEGE

To Bowden, having the opportunity to return home to coach his alma mater was like a miracle sent from Heaven. Therefore, he wasted no time in calling his good friend, James Sharman, the new Athletic Director, to give his reply.

But more importantly, one must understand how this miracle took place to grasp the impact it would later make on Bowden's life. It all began in 1957 when the new president of the University of Alabama, Dr. Frank Rose, hired away from Texas A&M a man named Bryant, to rebuild the Crimson Tide's football fortunes. Well, one year later, Dr. Leslie Wright, the new president of Howard College had similar visions. After all, Howard *was* the second largest Baptist school in the country, next to Baylor, which was a major college football power. So why couldn't Howard compete with the big leaguers?

Yet, there was a bit of divine assistance in the selection process. It seems that James Sharman, the Athletic Director, had just fired the previous coach and couldn't find a replacement. So like all good Baptists, he prayed over the matter, and when his heavenly meditation was finished, he glanced up to see on his desk a 1953 Howard yearbook, the same yearbook which listed little Bobby Bowden as an All-American quarterback selection. After seeing Bowden's picture and checking into the young coach's success, Sharman had no doubts who the man would be to bring their program out of the valley of despair and onto bigger and better things.

So Bowden packed his two older sons, Steve and Tommy, into the family station wagon and headed to Birmingham for an interview at Howard College and a brief visit with his and Ann's families.

When he arrived, Bowden found the firm commitment-to-winning that he knew would be needed to resurrect the program. Another big plus was Dr. Wright. He was the type of school administrator who knew the positive effects big time football would have on a school's alumni and student body. So, following a meeting of the minds and a thorough discussion of "this is what we've got to do to win around here again," Bowden, Sharman, and Wright shook hands; signed a contract; and began an era in the history of Howard College that the school would never again have the opportunity to experience.

8

Going Home

"There was one young man whose name kept appearing on the list whom I thought could really help us. He was Mal Moore, a reserve quarterback. But Coach Bryant would never let him go. He kept saying, 'Mal Moore is gonna be somebody that we'll all be proud of one day."

Building any new program from the beginning is tough, especially at Howard College. Yet like another coach, one headquartered in Tuscaloosa, Alabama, who was charged with a similar responsibility, Bobby Bowden went at his task with tremendous dedication and confidence. And as Paul Bryant had done at Maryland in 1946 with his merrymen of World War II misfits from the North Carolina Navy Pre-Flight School, Bowden brought along 13 junior college recruits who had the spirit of adventure within them. And knowing Bowden, that he was going to be a winner wherever he went, they wanted an opportunity to be in on the ground floor of something that was going to be *big*—something that was going to be *successful*.

"The first thing I did," Bowden later revealed, "was attend a coaching clinic in Tallahassee, Florida, where Tom Nugent, the FSU head coach, and Forest Evashevski, the Iowa head coach, were lecturing. Coach Evashevski took a liking to me real quickly, and soon invited me up to Iowa for spring training. They had just returned from beating a very good Cali-

(left to right) Bowden, Little All-America Bennie Storie, and Athletic Director James Sharman during awards celebration after 1959 season.

It was an exciting afternoon when Howard broke Sewannee's 14-game winning streak in 1959.

fornia team in the Rose Bowl that year. So I wasted no time in accepting their offer."

But Bowden's greatest growth of football knowledge was to come a lot closer to home, for the years that Bowden spent 60 miles to the southwest of Birmingham, in nearby Tuscaloosa, were years that would transfuse his knowledge of football with Bryant blood, the kind that won football games. And the long and exhaustive hours in the Alabama football office trading philosophies on football and talking about good clean living with Jerry Claiborne, Phil Cutchins, and Gene Stallings, all of them future head coaches, were years that would mold the man, Bowden, into a great coach.

"Every chance I had, I'd drive down to Tuscaloosa to visit with my good friend Gene Stallings, who always took his time to explain Alabama football philosophy to me.

"I'd usually get there by 10 A.M. and we'd sit there by the chalk board with guys like Sam Bailey, Jerry Claiborne, Phil Cutchins, Clem Gryska and Bryant, just talking football. Then by five or six in the evening we'd break up to go eat supper and continue talking football.

"I learned a lot of football just watching those guys work on the chalk board or on the field.

"Each Spring, Hayden Riley and Carney Laslie would prepare a list of players whom they had made a mistake on while recruiting and felt couldn't play at Alabama but deserved an opportunity to play somewhere else. I, in turn, was supposed to watch those kids in practice and later discuss their particular situation with Coach Bryant. If he thought a youngster wouldn't have an opportunity to play at Alabama, he'd usually suggest that the young man transfer to Howard.

"There was one young man whose name kept appearing on that list, whom I thought could really help us. He was Mal Moore, a reserve quarterback. But Coach Bryant would never let him go. He kept saying, 'Mal Moore is gonna be somebody that we'll all be proud of one day.'

"Coach Bryant was always a great judge of people because today, Mal Moore is his offensive co-ordinator and has won more football games and championships with the wishbone offense for Bryant than any other offensive assistant."

Bowden's first fall at the new Howard College campus on the side of Shades Mountain was monumental. All in all, the Bulldogs would have a three-man coaching staff: Walter Barnes (the basketball and track coach), Virgil Ledbetter (the baseball coach), and Bowden. And when practice started, he and his staff began the awesome chore of reformulating a once sacred winning football tradition.

Bowden, the fiesty new coach, had a plan . . . *why not build with youth?* So with fifteen returning lettermen and twenty-three new talented freshman recruits coming aboard, Bowden began to form the foundation of his new program.

"During fall practice we worked 'em hard trying to separate the football players from the guys who were just out there to look good. And the kids really worked hard, too. The kids who stayed after that first year were the ones who were willing to hit, and to pay the price that it takes to win football games."

Much of Bowden's youth movement centered around six freshmen, four sophomores, and a junior—guys like Bonwell Royal and Jimmy Thompson who played guard, Richard Finley and Bennie Storie who played tackle, Carl Shepherd at center, Buddy Bozeman and Don Coleman at end, Bobby Jackson and George Versprille at halfback, big Robert Lairsey at fullback and Joe Milazzo, an ex-Ramsey High ace who would throw for 1079 yards in nine games in 1959.

And beginning in September of 1959, Bowden and his Howard Bulldogs began their resurgence from the half-hidden shadows of the past and into the spotlight of small college football.

It all began in the season opener against Sewanee, sporting a long win streak and coached by Shirley Majors, the father of Tennessee Volunteer standout, Johnny Majors. The game was tough, but the men from Howard ended up whacking the Tigers, 20-0.

Then, *Bowden and Co.* reeled off a succession of victories over Maryville (14-0), Tennessee Tech (34-0), Milsaps (26-0),

Bowden's winning backfield at Howard (left to right) George Versprille, Joe Milazzo, Bob Lairsey, and Bobby Jackson.

In four seasons, Bowden went 31 and 6 with the Howard Bulldogs.

Southwestern (16-0), Livingston (24-0), University of Tennessee-Martin (14-13) and Troy State (20-18) with a single loss coming against always tough Mississippi College (26-7).

But the standout 8-1 record was to become the best in Howard's history, overshadowing the 7-1-2 set in 1935—the year Pat Harrison, the Snell boys, Norman Cooper, Herman Hodges, Harold Hill, and others tied a defending Rose Bowl Champion Alabama Crimson Tide, 7-7, and lost only to Mississippi State.

Yes, those were the glory days of an earlier Howard tradition. And the cornerstone of Howard athletics, both past and present, was built around that game in September of 1935, some time before any of Bowden's young Bulldogs were outfitted with helmet and shoulder pads for a first birthday or Christmas. Howard played Alabama, and Billy Bancroft was on the sidelines head-coaching his first Howard game against a Crimson Tide team which had done Stanford in at the Rose Bowl on January 1 with players like Howell and Hudson and Bryant.

And according to Bancroft, the football mentor who had established the tradition that Bowden was trying to rebuild, "Joe Riley (the Alabama halfback) had a bad knee and we threw behind him. We had Don Snell crossing over Ewing Harbin for our touchdown.

"Then Penry Penrod kicked the extra point. I also remember Paul Bryant dropping a pass out in the open (Paul Bryant does, too).

"They tied us. We didn't tie them."

Howard just wasn't supposed to be on the same field with Alabama. But on that immortal day, young Billy Bancroft would look across Denny Stadium and see Alabama's great coach, Frank Thomas, stunned and silent.

"What I remember most was Coach Hank Crisp after the game.

"Hank came over to our dressing room, and here was a big man. He congratulated everybody, and he brought the game ball with him.

" 'Here,' he said. 'I expect this will mean something to you some day.' "

Those were the days of Bancroft and Eubank and Cooper, and all of the others who were part of Howard at the time: a testimony to the fact that football was, and is, important to Howard.

For there was once a Howard in 1935, small and struggling . . . and under Wright, and Sharman and Bowden, there developed a new Howard, growing all of the time. They go together.

9

My Friend, Bart

"One day I phoned and asked Bart to come over to spring practice, watch us work out and talk some football. Kinda critique our program.
"He said, 'Sure, I'll be glad to.'"

It was a bright day in Birmingham as "the new look" Howard College and its up-and-coming football program had stepped forward into the bigtime winners circle with a fancy 9-1 record, including a win over Gordon Military Academy in the post season Textile Bowl in Langdale, Georiga.

Speaking before a crowd of 260 who had turned out to honor the 1959 football team at a banquet in the school's dining hall, Dr. Leslie Wright, the school's president, proclaimed, "We are not trying to build a major football power here at Howard College, but we do believe as the institution grows that all segments of it should move together.

"Hence, we will keep our athletic teams in step with academic strides which we will be striving to make toward making Howard one of the outstanding schools in the South."

And as Dr. Wright, young and competent, a former player and coach himself and now a staunch supporter of Bobby Bowden football, continued his talk, he hailed Head Coach Bowden as "a Little All-American who has shown he can teach what he practiced in his days as a player at Howard" for the team's success.

Assistant Coaches, Virgil Ledbetter and Walter Barnes, pose with Bowden and a gruesome pair of Howard Bulldogs.

Bowden became known as a jittery genius during this years at Howard.

"Our camera man always did like those ballet poses."

Then Bowden got up to address the audience and lauded his players and assistants Virgil Ledbetter and Walter Barnes for the team's fast start in his first year as the Bulldogs' head coach.

He said, "You boys had a mighty good attitude. We put you through hard work, and you stayed with it."

After that, Bowden made 10 awards to players who had led Howard's resurgance. Among those were sophomore tackle Benny Storie who received a Williamson trophy as Howard's first Little All-American since Bowden was so honored in 1952.

But after all of the festooning, the warm handshakes, and the backslapping, Bowden, the determined coach, quickly cast aside any further plaudits. For tomorrow, the next day, was a new year and a new season. It was time to go back to work. Already, bigger league Georgetown had been added to the 1960 schedule, replacing Tennessee Tech, and Carson-Newman was signed for 1961-62. Soon, attempts would be made to add eastern power Washington & Lee. Definitely, bigger and better things were happening there in the valley below Shades Mountain.

"In the spring of 1960, I began to discover the passing attack which would later become my bread and butter. And all of the credit goes to Bart Starr.

"Bart was just beginning to make good as a professional with Coach Lombardi and the Green Bay Packers. And in the off-season he'd always come to Birmingham to work with an automobile dealership which he later bought and made successful.

"One day I phoned and asked Bart to come over to spring practice, watch us work out, and talk some football. Kinda critique our program.

"He said, 'Sure, I'll be glad to.'

"During spring practice the year before, I ususally had to coach the team myself since Virgil Ledbetter would be handling baseball and Walter Barnes would be coaching track. So that left me by myself with football and we'd usually have to split practice up into two sessions of 1½ hours each just to be able to get a proper work out.

"Well, Bart came over and I gave him a pair of sweats and cleats and we're walking out to the practice field and I asked him, 'Why don't you take the quarterbacks and work with them and I'll work with the receivers.'

"He said, 'That sounds like a great idea.' And when practice was over Bart and I got together and discussed the strengths and weaknesses of the offensive and defensive personnel.

"Now, I was really impressed with the coaching tips that he had given me. So the next day I got on the phone and called him again about some advice and he volunteered to come over to practice again.

"Well, that went on for nearly five weeks, and Bart was doing a great job imparting wisdom to our youthful squad and instilling them with the necessary confidence that they needed to grow as a football team. And by the time the Blue-White Spring Game came, Bart and I began discussing strategy on how to get a true test of how the squad had progressed.

"He suggested a spring game based on a running attack vs. a passing attack, which I quickly agreed to. So Bart took the passing attack with Joe Milazzo and Buddy Bozeman and I took the running attack headed up by Bobby Jackson, Billy Hurst, and George Versprille. Let me tell you, Bart had his side ready and they beat us 22-18. I knew then that the passing game was going to be in my future for a long time."

And in the next three years, Bobby Bowden football began to grow. And new Howard College continued to build. More dormitories were added and Seibert Hall, the 4,000 seat gymnasium was built, with almost unlimited intramural room and a swimming pool in the basement, too. And there was a 6,000 seat stadium built into the hillside with lights for T.V. games and Tifton-57 bermuda grass to match the big league caliber play. It was as if Robert Browning was thinking of Howard College when he wrote, "The best is yet to be."

Yes, Major Harwell G. Davis and Alabama's Baptists did a world of dreaming when they left the Old Howard College

Bowden and Co. turned the program around and renewed an old tradition of winning at Howard.

standing lonely in East Lake and climbed across the mountain to develop the Howard that is. But Wright and Sharman
and the students of Howard had youth and determination on
their side—and leadership and support, enthusiasm and
desire.

And in three seasons the mighty Bulldogs had won 24 big
games and lost only 4 while continuing their rise to the top.
In 1963, little Howard climbed out of the small college class
twice to upend Chattanooga and Furman in stunning upsets
and finished with a 7-1 record and a berth in the prestigous
small college Golden Isle Bowl.

It is ironic, however, that the Bulldogs lost their only game
to the only team which they didn't scout, Delta State. But
Howard's scouting system was without a budget so extra
measures had to be made.

"After the first game of the season against Chattanooga,
we had an open date. So Virgil Ledbetter and I formulated a
plan such that we could scout all of our opponents for the remainder of the season except Delta State.

"The plan was based on Ledbetter driving to Biloxi, Mississippi, to scout the University of Mexico against Southern
Mississippi on Thursday. Then on Friday he caught Mississippi College playing Arkansas State in Jackson, and on
Saturday he'd watch Louisiana College playing Troy.

"Now, we also were to play both Furman and Wofford
that year, so I went to see them play on that Saturday and
then traveled to see Carson-Newman play Appalachian that
night. Boy, what a trip!"

Fatiguing, perhaps, but what a successful scouting expedi-
tion it turned out to be; for in 1962, Howard beat Mexico,
Louisiana College, Furman, Carson-Newman, Mississippi
College, and Wofford. Unfortunately, for Howard, neither
Bowden nor Ledbetter could get to Delta State. And as for
Chattanooga or Furman, neither or them requested an en-
core on the schedule after losing that year.

10

West Virginia

> *"Well, his dad was from the old country and he wrote the boy back and said, 'Son, I just got this letter from Mr. Carlen and Mr. Carlen is a nice guy, a good guy, and he says you've been doing this and you've been doing that and if I hear of you doing it again I'm going to come down there and bash your head in.'"*

In four short years, Bobby Bowden and a hard working coaching staff had brought little Howard College from the outhouse to the penthouse of small college football. Even SEC opponents considered the up-start Baptist school a formable foe when Mississippi State asked them to join their schedule beginning in September, 1963.

But Bowden had a desire to be the head coach of a major college team and little Howard was never going to be anything more than a great "minor leaguer." So when FSU head mentor, Bill Peterson came knocking at Bowden's door for his services in the winter of 1963, the offer was awful tempting.

"I had been with Darrell Royal, the head coach at Texas, that day. We had been at the Thomas Jefferson Hotel with the Birmingham Touchdown Club when a telephone call came for me. On the other end of the line was Bill Peterson whom I had met at a Touchdown Club function in Atlanta."

"He said, 'Bobby, I want you to come down to Tallahassee and visit with me about a job working with my offense.'

"Well, I was really excited yet didn't want to tell anybody, especially since I was under contract to Howard."

"That night, Darrell and I drove to Anniston, Alabama for a speaking engagement and it snowed the entire way. Finally we got there and checked into a room which they had waiting for us."

"We had only been there thirty minutes when the phone began to ring. It was a newspaper man from Birmingham."

"He asked, 'Coach Bowden, what's this I hear about you going to Florida State.' Quite surprised to find out how fast news travels, I explained that it was only for an interview and he agreed to keep the story quiet. The next day, however, the headline read: BOWDEN LEAVING HOWARD FOR FSU.

"I knew then that I'd really be in trouble with Dr. Wright about this, so I went to see him first thing after the newspaper story broke. He was understanding, too. He told me how to use the words 'no comment' in the future and reassured me that Howard wanted me to take the FSU job if I thought it'd eventually get me a major head coaching job.

"I guess Dr. Wright knew all of the time that my dream would come true. And for his wonderful support, I'll always be indebted."

Soon thereafter, Bowden did get the job at FSU. And in 1964 Peterson, the football staff and the Seminole squad put together the greatest season in FSU football history to that date by going 9-1-1 and whipping highly favored Oklahoma in the Gator Bowl.

The next year, following the 1965 season, Georgia Tech assistant under legendary Bobby Dodd, Jim Carlen, was named the new head coach at West Virginia. And the Mountaineer head mentor wasted no time in luring away the coach who helped mold quarterback Steve Tensi, and wide receiver, Fred Biletnikoff, into an awesome scoring weapon, and who had made the Seminole attack a team to be feared.

Quickly, Bowden accepted the job as offensive co-ordinator for Carlen and headed to the coal-filled mountains of West Virginia. Little did Bowden know that this sleepy paced

Enthusiasm has always been a part of Bowdens winning philosophy.

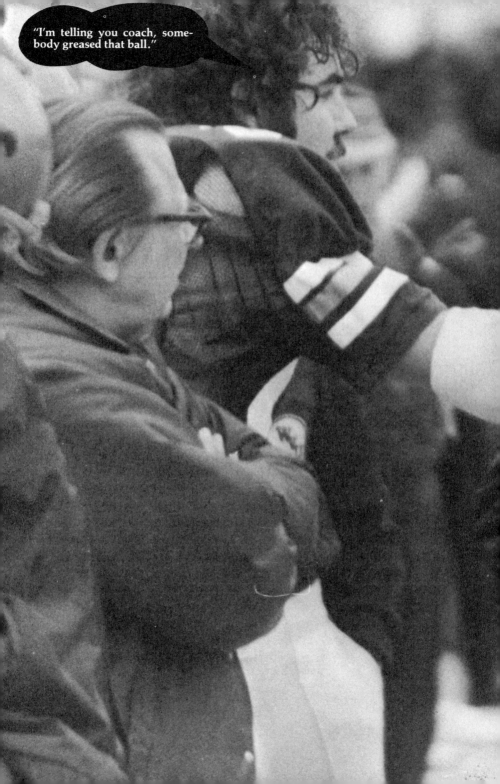

"Let's take it this way, baby."

"I owe a lot to Bill Peterson for giving me the opportunity to join a major college team."

state would be his home for the next ten years. But it would, and like any place that he'd been to before—the program would improve and they'd become big time winners.

*   *   *

"When I went to West Virginia, I learned a lot about recruiting, especially traveling through those coal fields and winding roads. I drove five hours to pick up this player and drove him back to West Virginia for an official visit. It was because of that trip that we got him. I was about to go to sleep while driving back, so I asked the young man if he could drive.

"He said, 'Yeah.'

"I said, 'Are you sure? Do you have a license?'

"He said, 'I'm taking student driving.'

"Well, he convinced me he could drive and so I let him drive back. And and hour later he drove right up the back of a truck—right up the back. Evidently, he had started to pass this truck and was unable to, so here I am sitting on the right hand side sleeping with my head up against the window and he runs underneath the back of a truck and the big truck breaks the glass right beside my head, pops the aerial, breaks the windshield and if he had been just two inches over it might have hit my head.

"Well, we pulled over and I asked if anybody was hurt. Fortunately, there wasn't. Now, I didn't want to report the accident because my recruit didn't have his license. And the man driving the truck had been drinking so we got lucky.

"Later, I found out that the young man's license had been suspended and he knew that if he got into trouble, he'd lose his license. I reckon that's one reason we got him to come to West Virginia.

"When I finally got to be the head coach at West Virginia we were recruiting this kid who was noted the most out-standing football player in the state. He lived way back up in a hollow, 20 miles outside of Charleston, West Virginia on the longest dirt road in the state. He was really great. Nearly everybody offered him a scholarship and it got down between Maryland and West Virginia.

"His dad was sheriff of this little community. He was a mean guy, too. But we finally convinced his dad—the sheriff—after we got the Captain to tell the sheriff that if his son went to West Virginia he'd let him off every Saturday so he could go watch his son play. And if his son went to Maryland he'd get nothing. So the Mother decided she wanted him to go to West Virginia and the Dad said he wanted him to go there. But it still wasn't signing day. And if somebody walks in there the next day he's liable to convince the kid otherwise.

"Now, Jerry Claiborne is supposed to come in the next day to visit the boy one more time. I looked at the dad and said. 'You're not going to let that coach see him are you?

"He said, 'I'll shoot him.' And he might have done it.

"Anyway Jerry never did come, but until today, I still think that that guy would have shot him. He was that bad.

"Another time, we signed this kid out of Western Pennsylvania whose dad was a coal miner, and an Italian, and the kid had broke a couple of training rules and Coach Carlen wrote the boy's daddy and told him that his son had done the following violations and if he does it again 'I'm going to have to kick him off the football team.'

"Well, his dad was from the old country and he wrote the boy back and said, 'Son, I just got this letter from Mr. Carlen and Mr. Carlen is a nice guy, a good guy, and he says you've been doing this and you've been doing that and if I hear of you doing it again I'm going to come down there and bash your head in . . . Love, Dad.'

"Might have been a little mafia—I don't know. But I'll guarantee you his son straightened up and finished. There were tough kids up there—that's what I like about it."

"My career at West Virginia, however, was not all glory and happiness. In 1974, our team went 4-7 and it was my first losing season as head coach. Boy, times were tough then.

"I walked out on campus one day and I saw myself hung in

THE YEAR OF THE MOUNTAINEER ON CABLE CHANNEL NINE

HOME SCHEDULE
Sept. 22 – VA. TECH.
Oct. 6 – INDIANA
Oct. 13 – PITT
Nov. 10 – BOSTON COLLEGE
Nov. 17 – VIRGINIA

WATCH TAPED REPLAY – TUES. – 10:30 PM

BOBBY BOWDEN
Head Coach

"We had some big years at West Virginia."

cotterman

effigy. You talk about an ego deflator, there's just nothing worse. What do you tell your kids when you see something like that. Do you say, 'Look, there's Daddy hanging over there?'

"Those were the hardest years of my life, then. And I learned a real valuable lesson. I learned just how much people love you when you're winning, and just how vicious some folks will get when you're down. I learned about the fickleness of fans, and I learned to take care of myself and my family."

Bowden's career hit the pits in 1974, his fifth season as head man at West Virginia. The top two quarterbacks were just a few of the starters injured. The Mountaineers finished 4-7, Bowden's first losing season as a head coach.

"Dad didn't hear or see half the stuff that went on," said Tommy Bowden, a flanker on the team. "At halftime of the basketball games, I'd be in the stands, and the crowd would be cheering 'Bobby Bowden blanks' or some kind of obscenity.

"They had signs on campus and in store windows about what a lousy coach my father was. They wouldn't walk up and say anything to my face, but most of 'em didn't know I was his son.

"It was pretty bad for me. I took it personal. And that's one thing my dad taught me: Keep your head, keep on doing what you think is right and things will work themselves out.

"He never showed a thing; he never folded."

It was, Bowden says, "the fair-weather fans" who were the tormentors. They regularly hung him in effigy. He received a death threat over the phone.

"It was a horrible year," Ann Bowden said. "I'd have to try to read his moods when he came home. When things were going bad, he'd be tight.

"It made it kind of tough on me because I'm the worst fan of all. Every time we touched the ball, I wanted a touchdown. I'd have to feel him out and find the right thing to say. Sometimes, I'd ask him about a play and why it didn't work and he'd say, 'You're just like the rest of the fans.' But he

"At West Virginia, we went for youth at quarterback."

"... and at linebacker, too."

never meant it and would always say he was sorry right after it.

"They were tough times."

The toughest times, however, were those long Saturday night–Sunday morning drives from Morgantown to Charleston to tape his TV highlights show.

Because there were no TV studios in Morgantown, Bobby and Ann, plus the host of the show, would trudge to the car at midnight—after the obligatory postgame party at the Bowden home—and start the four-hour drive south.

"We'd check into a motel and get about an hour or so of sleep, get up at 5, tape the show, then turn around and drive back," Bowden said. "It was pretty hard to smile and be cheerful after you lost, and your eyes felt like they were about to fall out."

Bowden likes to say he decided to leave West Virginia for Florida State in the winter of '76 after he "slipped on the ice and fell on my elbow," but he had made up his mind long before that, and his hatred of cold weather played but a small part in his decision.

He had enough of the personal rip-jobs by some of his tormentors of the press, the back-stabbing and the jeers of fickle fans. It just made him mad enough to vow that if he got a good job offer he felt he had every right to accept it.

So, before his '75 team went 9-3 and beat N.C. State in the Peach Bowl, he knew that would be his last year. "I didn't want to give anyone the satisfaction of knowing I was leaving with my tail between my legs."

11

Mission Possible

The licks sounded awful, like pairs of pick-up trucks hitting head on. Florida State students, wandering past the practice field, have only recently gotten used to the hitting they hear from across the hedges as their football team works in the afternoons.

But this is Florida State, the national power, the one Bobby Bowden promised and delivered.

Not so long ago, free-spirited players roamed these fields in loose work-outs, preparing for little more than another humiliating defeat.

"When I first came here, you were sort of ashamed to admit you were a football player," claimed fifth-year Seminole Wally Woodham, who with Jimmy Jordan formed FSU's famed tandem of passing quarterbacks in 1979.

But that was before Bowden arrived as a coach, before heavy discipline and hard-hitting, before the national ranking, the TV deals, and big bowl money, before the undercurrent of planning got underway to make a perennial national power out of the one-time weakest sister of major college football in the South.

It all started with the arrival of this Seminole Savior in 1976 from the coal-mining mountain tops of West Virginia. In

*four short seasons FSU and Bobby Bow-
den's brand of football had reached the
trumpeted grandiose glory of big-time college football.*

*It wasn't easy, but they got there—his
way.*

"When John Bridgers, the Athletic Director of Florida
State, approached me down at the American Bowl in Tampa
about the possibility of taking the head coaching job at his
school, I could think of only two jobs that could have been
worse - 1) Being elected mayor of Atlanta shortly after Sher-
man left town, or 2) being the general who volunteers to
replace George Custer during the last siege at Little Big Horn.
Things there were just about that bad.

"But Bridgers was persistent and that got me to thinking
real serious about Florida State. After all, how could someone lose while recruiting in the state of Florida? There was
just no way.

"Yet, there were other things to be considered too. Was
Florida State ready to make a *commitment* to build a winning program? Were they ready to raise the financial support, add on to the stadium and do the things that are done at
Arkansas, Notre Dame or Texas?

"When Bridgers said, 'Yes,' my answer became easy.

"The reasoning was really quite simple. John Bridgers was
a Birmingham boy looking for a good head coach and I was a
Birmingham boy, too, who happended to be head coaching a
winning program at West Virginia up in the *cold* weather
country. I hated cold weather.

"At the time, however, there were a few other gentlemen
in the coaching picture at Florida State, first-class guys from
winning programs up north. I suppose they just wanted out
of the ice and snow, too.

"Now, don't take me wrong. I never went after the job at

(left to right) Bill Peterson, Bowden and Don Faurot during coaches luncheon in the mid-sixties.

Hollywood current box office hit Burt Reynolds, was once a Seminole.

Florida State. They came to me. As a matter of fact, I never got any job that I went after. I had missed out on the Wake Forest job while an assistant at West Virginia. Same thing with Baylor. So when I signed that contract at Florida State, it was the result of pure *fate*.

"Then, when the bowl game was over, the contract signed and the hoopla all settled down, I knew that *we*—the players, the staff, the faculty, the alumni and fans—would need a common cause to rally our program onward and build a good foundation, which is always crucial.

"Well, I got to thinking for a while, trying to figure out what would turn this program around. I knew that we would need a cause that people would fight for and would be willing to 'lay it on the line,' day-in and day-out, for four years of their life.

"Then it finally came. Bob Harbison, who had been with the program since it began at Florida State and whom I had retained to be my offensive line coach, came in one morning to brief me on the recruiting picture in Miami and South Florida. He told me how well the University of Florida was doing and that we'd be lucky to come out of there having signed anyone.

"I knew then and there, what our common cause had to be. Beating that other school down it Gainesville just had to become our rallying point. More than that, it had to become an obsession, something our people would live and die for.

"You see, 1975-76 had been the year of the Gators, and in

"When I came to FSU they promised me plenty of warm weather. Yet, against North Texas State in 1976, we played in 3 inches of snow."

a state where football runs a close second to God and beautiful sun-tanned girls in skimpy bikinis—depending upon where you're from—that meant a great deal.

"In bars. In locker rooms. From rathskeller to rathskeller. In sorority and fraternity houses—anywhere really—Florida State fans were always considered second-class.

"Florida high school players didn't want to go to Florida State; that was suicide. At that point, the Gators had their pick of the recruiting litter, if a high schooler wanted to remain in state.

"And if overall records weren't enough comparison, Gator fans needed only to point out the final tally of the six previous encounters from 1970 to 1975. Florida got six, FSU—zip.

"At that point, getting down on Florida State football was the most popular pasttime in Florida, second only to getting down on Richard Nixon.

"But I believed differently. Eventually, so would everyone else.

"That belief started with the guys that I selected for my staff. Coach Bryant had taught me while I was head coaching at Howard that in order to win, to build your kind of program, you must surround yourself with winners, guys who are eager-eyed, hard-working, and hungry enough to want the same things you do.

"Well there were three guys on Darrell Mudra's staff who I thought were hungry enough to aid the cause—Bob Harbison, Jim Gladden, and Gene McDowell, a former All-America at Florida State. Bob had joined the FSU staff in 1948 in its second year of college football. He had been there when Don Veller, Bill Peterson and Larry Jones had built winning programs. Winning meant something to Bob Harbison.

"Then there was Jim Gladden and Gene McDowell. Those guys were so motivated that there was no way that I could let them go. If I had told them that running through a brick wall would help us win—they would have done it. No questions asked.

"From my staff at West Virginia I brought in Jerry Bruner, a former FSU man, to work with the offensive line and George Henshaw, the first player I ever recruited while at West Virginia, to coach my defensive people. And to coach all of those Florida speedsters that we would recruit, I brought in Kent Schoolfield from the high school ranks. All three were young guys and eager to learn. I knew that I could count on them.

"But most importantly, I needed two guys from established winning programs to coordinate my offense and my defense. These were guys who had been there before, guys who had had that sweet taste of success. From Bill Dooley's staff at North Carolina I enlisted Jack Stanton to run the defense. And on offense George Haffner was persuaded to leave Pittsburgh, Johnny Majors, and Tony Dorsett to come south and make the offense click.

"All of them had one common bond—they wanted to win."

12

Winning — My Way

There were a few snickers, but mostly the room became quiet—very quiet. And this group of young men began to listen with interest as Bowden continued. He has something of importance to tell. And seizing this oppoutunity, Bowden, the great coach of winning teams and young men of outstanding character, became Bowden the great teacher. He had a lesson to preach and on this very important day in January it poured out—with impact and new courage.

The day was out of the book on January—cold, gray, very wet. A day of unusual appearance at Florida State University.

But it was more than it seemed to be, this January 16th, year of 1976.

Bobby Bowden was out of bed at 5:30 A.M. as is his way. Like the other early birds, he could say to himself. "The nights are getting shorter," when the first pale light comes to Tallahassee.

It was getting good day by the time he came to his office at 6:15 and started attending to a stack of letters ranging from speaking requests to inquiries from assistant coaches looking to come South to this sunshine state capital.

At eight o'clock, the secretaries and other members of his newly assembled staff began to arrive. Then the chatter of

Bowden has always been a man of many expressions.

and many emotions.

typewriters and clicking of film projectors were soon underway as the office of Bobby Bowden's football program came to life.

At 9:30 he met with Bob Harbison, Jim Gladden, George Henshaw, Jerry Bruner, Kent Schoolfield, George Haffner, and the rest of the men on his Florida State University football-coaching staff.

"We're going to build a foundation here, so stay organized and keep things simple," he told them about their new program. "Also, let's get something accomplished."

At 10:30, he was back at his desk; at noon he lunched. Then at 1:30, he stood before all young people, football players who would become great men, and said what he had to say.

"Gentlemen, let me explain the importance of why we're all here together."

Pausing, then looking to both sides of the room for a brief moment, Bowden continued. "First of all, we've got to have a basic understanding of who's in charge around here. There can never be a question of that.

"Well, I am the new guy around here. I'm the head coach. And in the past three years *your* Florida State football team has managed to win only four games and in the meantime lost 29. Ya'll have tried it your way, and where did it get you? Nowhere. Now, I think I know how to win. And from now on at Florida State we're gonna do things my way. If you don't like it, then hit the door. Go somewhere else. Because if winning doesn't mean something to you then we don't need you. From now on it's going to be an honor to wear a garnet jersey and represent *Florida State University.* We're gonna win again at Florida State."

There were a few snickers, but mostly the room became quiet—very quiet. And this group of young men began to listen with interest as Bowden continued. He had something of importance to tell. And seizing this opportunity, Bowden, the great coach of winning teams and young men of outstanding character, became Bowden the great teacher. He had a lesson to preach and on this very important day in January it poured out—with impact and new courage.

"Now, I think that we can turn this program around at Florida State. But, gentlemen, it's going to take a big effort by everyone. We're going to have to push ourselves harder than ever before. We're gonna have to make sacrifices—give up individual goals in order to reach a much bigger team goal. But we can do it—WE CAN WIN AT FLORIDA STATE."

The room was completely quiet, all eyes focused on the man up-front as Bowden pulled out a sheet of paper and continued, "Vince Lombardi, the great coach of the Green Bay Packers, once described that glorious feeling that winners have—the kind of feeling that none of you have enjoyed while at Florida State. He said, 'I firmly believe that man's finest hour, his greatest fulfillment to all he holds dear . . . is that moment when he has worked his heart out in a good cause and lies exhausted on the field-victorious!'

"Gentlemen, that will be our goal. That will be the feeling that we all want to achieve—to feel like a winner, to be able to walk around this campus with the satisfaction of knowing that 'Yes, we can win.' And in order to get that feeling of confidence, and to begin winning football games, then some things around here have got to change.

"First of all, we've got to develop a winning attitude and that means self-discipline because self-discipline wins football games. And that's our goal at Florida State—to win football games."

Bowden now appeared in full control of the situation at hand, speaking with a confidence that comes from success. He had a refreshed look of calmness about him. And as his team watched him, each player received in his eyes the full candle power usually reserved for intense moments. But his was a special time—when a little, big man stood tall.

"Now in order to build a winning program and develop self-discipline we've got to make some rules around here. And that means making a commitment to ourselves and to each other that we're going to follow those rules.

"So let's start with hair. I'm not going to ask you to look like Kojaks, but we *are* going to keep it neat and we *are* going to look like football players.

"We're also gonna *go* to class and *get-up* for breakfast. And there's *not* gonna be any room on this team for individuals who've got to smoke and drink. If you do then you're gonna be gone.

"Next, we're gonna ask that you attend church regularly and write your Mom and Dad. It'll *mean* a lot to them, and more to you over the years."

Slowly, head-coach Bobby Bowden was revealing his plan—his road map for success. Soon, he would take these young men assembled before him, who appeared to be a group of misfits and losers, and gradually change them into a slashing, hard-driving, aggressive squad.

"So, gentlemen, what is sacrifice?" Bowden asked as he pointed at a sophomore running back nearby. Pausing, as the frightened youngster gave a blank expression, Bowden then continued. "It's having a little pride in yourself to not be like the average students. You've gotta outwork them— you've gotta have a desire to excel.

"Sacrifice also means displaying a winning attitude, looking and acting like an athlete, recognizing the attributes of other students, giving 'em a pat-on-the-back, shaking their hands and looking 'em in the eye while doing it. Sacrifice means, 'Yes, sir' and 'No, sir' to your supervisors.

"But remember, it takes *class* to come back in the fourth quarter and win, but if we've sacrificed—we can do it.

"There won't be too many other training rules, just use your head. Try to eat and sleep good. Be on time for meetings. And try to have a goal every day—try to get better. If you have a bad day, don't lose your confidence. Just try to improve day-to-day.

"Now, gentlemen, listen-up on this final point. We represent a lot of people . . . our families, our friends back at home and, very importantly, we represent Florida State University. And as a team I want to point this out to you. YOU'RE NOT ORDINARY—YOU'RE NOT AVERAGE—

On the sidelines Bowden gives instructions to his quarterback in 1976 win against Boston College.

Bowden and his second love—golf.

YOU'RE SOMETHING SPECIAL—and I don't want you to ever forget that. And since you are something special, then I know that as a team, WE CAN WIN—if you put something extra into it every day, and a little bit extra into a game.

"Gentlemen, we have a tough road ahead, and we've got to be both mentally and physically tough to make it. But if we're prepared in the proper manner, then when the time comes—winning will take care of itself."

Before closing, Bowden added, "My office door will always be open to you. If I'm on the phone or with someone, then give me a minute and I'll be happy to talk with you about anything."

The meeting ended. The room was completely quiet, all eyes focused on the man up-front as Bowden turned to his left to exit through the big steel panelled door that led to his office. All the talk was done.

And in a few weeks, spring practice would begin. Then his new team would come in garnet and gold and white jerseys, the FSU Seminoles of 1976, big, strong, and looking hungry and needing to learn some lessons, and wanting to, it was presumed.

The work was just beginning. But a dedicated Bobby Bowden, the FSU coach who once was an All-America football player, would join them on the difficult road back to prominence.

And this overcast day in January, this special day in the life of Bobby Bowden, could not be considered ordinary for him, for those who would work and play for him, for those who watched. It was a day to be remembered many years hence, a feeling that everything would be better right away, real soon.

Finally, Florida State was going to be a winner once again.

13

The New Regime

When Bobby Bowden arrived in Tallahassee, he found a football program awaiting the death bed of Old Father Time. Even the grave marker for the three previous seasons had been set. It read 4-29.

But Bowden never faltered. Instead, he poured both heart and soul into Tallahassee and FSU and released a flair of energy and zeal that quickly erased the long set-in apathy of earlier lost-cause regimes.

Suddenly, people came out of the woodwork to support the once-mighty Seminoles. People who were not even alumni, those who simply loved the role of an underdog, began joining the cause.

Yes, Horatio Alger had been reborn.

"It used to be that Florida State football coaches were viewed upon like the cowboy who walked into a saloon to order a drink on a Friday afternoon, only to find out that in the meantime his horse outside had been painted. After inspecting the damages, the cowboy quickly re-entered the saloon.

"Alright you guys," the angry cowboy shouts, "Who painted my horse!"

About that time, in comes the meanest looking gunfighter that the cowboy has ever seen.

He says, 'I did it. Now, what are you going to do about it?'

FSU mascots, The Seminole Warrior, and Renegade.

"Suddenly frightened by this awesome sight, the cowboy replies: "I just wanted to let you know that it needs a second coat."

"That's the way football coaching at Florida State used to be," Bobby Bowden explained. "We were always the little guy . . . second class. But things were going to change. They had to.

"First of all, it started with *attitude:* The boys had to believe they could win. That was the hardest thing to overcome. The on-the-surface attitude was nothing, but underneath was something else. What players were thinking deep down inside was the *real* problem.

"I don't believe I convinced too many people the first year. Sure, everyone talked like winners, but when we got out there in the trenches with them, one could tell they were thinkin: 'There's no way we're gonna win.'

"But what else could one expect at Florida State? After all, that's the way the ball had bounced around there for a long time. Yet, they, the players, had to take the big step. THEY had to go out and want to win. And I, as the head coach, had to tell them that they COULD win . . . THEY COULD! Then when the little things started to happen that gives a team the feeling of accomplishment, that makes them feel like a winner, all of a sudden they begin thinking, "My goodness, this might be the right way to do things."

"So, when we had that first meeting with the players, the weeding out process began. My thoughts, of course, were to go in there and tell them this is the way it's gonna be—we're going to do things my way.

"Walking in that room that eventful day required all of the fortitude that I could gather. But I had to. That first difficult step just had to be taken—they had to be challenged.

"So I told them, 'Ya'll are the ones that have been losing around for years. Ya'll are the losers. Ya'll can't do it your way and win. Now, I think I know how to WIN so this is gonna be how we do things—my way. And if you don't like it, you can leave. Go somewhere else.' I know some of the comments I heard were, 'Who does he think he is?' and that sort of thing. A few left but very few of them tested us.

"Somewhere amidst all of this, too, was our game plan, the foundation upon which our program was to be built. And meeting together hours upon long, grueling hours during the month of January, we finally developed the plan that we would install while at Florida State. Each member of the staff pledged to each other to stay within this framework and win, or die, with these fundamentals.

"The heart of the program, or course, would be bigger than any other coach or player, and we were determined to put the *team* first. Any player or staff member who would not, or could not, comply would be considered dead weight—they'd just have to go.

"Now, looking back, I feel very strongly that this approach has been the guts of our success while at Florida State; it isn't foolproof, magic, or 100 percent effective, but these were the principles that we believed in as a staff. This was our foundation.

"The assistant coaches were most important in developing this chemistry that underlines all winning programs. On our staff, it all began with hiring coaches who put the welfare of FSU and the players we coached ahead of everything else. For there was a much deeper responsibility to these young men that we would coach than just their football productivity at Florida State. After all, football lasts for only four years for 94% of all college athletes and then they are confronted by what to do with the rest of their lives. Our program was founded upon the principles of helping these young men find help academically and spiritually along with the physical development they got from playing football. As a team, we were going to study together, play together, and pray together, each man according to his own desire. To us, this type of program could win in more ways than just on the football field.

"But to win consistently on the field each year, we had to make a *commitment* to the type of young man that could help us win at Florida State. Those requirements fell into five

Keith Jones, 28, and Bobby Butler, 21,
stuck together when injuries devastated
the defensive backfield in 1978.

Bowden and Florida Head Coach, Charlie Pell, pose for gag photo in summer of 1979.

areas: 1) physical ability, 2) academic potential, 3) character, 4) dependability, and 5) ambition.

" Physical *ability*, of course, is the first thing we look for in an athlete because without it Florida State cannot compete on the national level to which we aspire. We felt that in order to win, and win big time, we would need players who could play for the Oklahomas, the Southern Cals and the Notre Dames. And one thing was for sure—we were not going to be satisfied until we could compete with those types of people.

"Second, we were going to check transcripts for academic potential because we wanted young men who could think and who would be with us through their senior year and have the desire to earn a degree. I later learned while coaching the East team at the Japan Bowl in Toyko what *brains* could do for a kid.

"In the Japan Bowl, as part of their rules, three Japanese youngsters are required to be placed on each team. So I said, "O.K.," and they proceeded to give me their three All-Stars, the biggest being a 5'8", 170 lb. tackle. On game day, I wasn't required to play any of my Japanese imports but all three of them had practiced very hard and had deserved to see some playing time. And when it was over, I never regretted it one bit, for those guys, who were all small enough to get killed on the field, had played a game of error-free football. I learned then that brains will always help you to win.

"Then, of course, there is *character*, which is definitely the most important attribute that a young man must possess. It doesn't matter if he is an All-America or a Rhodes Scholar, or both, if his character is questionable then we don't need him.

"Next, is *dependability*. One of the greatest examples of dependability occurred in 1979 when the Pittsburgh Pirates won the World Series. They said it was because of a team spirit which brought them together and rallied them to victory. That special esprit de corps was called "family," and what greater symbol is there for team togetherness than a family.

"The game of football is probably one of life's greatest teachers about dependability. It requires eleven young men on a football field to depend upon the other ten to help get a job done. And if every guy on the team does his job then that team is going to win.

"Dependability is the fulfillment of an obligation. It's also saying, "I'm going to show-up on time and then doing it. It's saying, "I'm going to play football—not chase cheerleaders." Dependability is also saying, "I'm going to do my job whatever the price."

"But physical ability, brains, character and dependability aren't going to win football games unless a youngster has the much needed *ambition*. If our staff at FSU could recruit players that wanted more than anything to be 'a great team' then we would have it made. There would be no need to motivate them. Instinctively, they would just want to do the things a great team will do. They'll study hard, they'll give the maximum effort on every play—they will *will* themselves to win games that ordinary teams would probably have lost.

"My favorite player with ambition was #51 of the Chicago Bears, Dick Butkus. He was one of those guys who made you ache all over when he tackled you. Butkus took great pride in being the toughest football player in the NFL.

"Once, while speaking to a football banquet in Baltimore, Maryland, I had the fine privilege of sitting next to Johnny Unitis, the great quarterback of the Baltimore Colts. I remember asking Johnny what was the most exciting moment that ever happened to him while in professional football.

"Well, he laughed and then replied, 'I've played nearly twenty years in the NFL, but the most exciting moment in my career had to be against the Chicago Bears when I had a pass intercepted by the Bears. It was Butkus.

" 'Naturally, I had to do something that most quarterbacks hate to do—move over and make the tackle. Anyway, I started to make my move and then I see my target. He was moving like a bull, snorting fire out of his nose and ears.

" 'Finally,' Unitis added, 'We hit head on, my headgear into that big #51 and big Butkus knocked me out of bounds while he went on to score. I thought he had killed me but he hadn't.'

"Yes, Dick Butkus was, in my opinion, the greatest linebacker in the NFL, and his greatest asset was that desire, that ambition to be the best, whatever the sacrifice. Recruiting young men to Florida State with that kind of ambition became our goal. We knew that if that could be accomplished, then winning would be only a matter of time at Florida State."

Doing it Bobby Bowden's way. Yes, that was the first major lesson. And sounding like a good ol' country boy, but sporting the serious football winning beliefs of Knute Rockne, Bowden began to make ready his troops like the general of an underdog army. Soon, people would begin getting excited.

Yet, continuing his rapid pace, Bobby Bowden kept building the cornerstone to a new FSU program. Alumnus and ex-football player Burt Reynolds would later address an autographed picture to Bowden with the inscription, "You are the One."

Yes, Bowden was the one.

14

Coming Back

Florida State 37, Florida 9 - December 3, 1977.

Roger Overby's eyes flamed. Only three months prior, he'd been fifth string, forgotten and wanted to quit. Today, he was a star. The little receiver fiercely clutched a game ball emblematic of three touchdown catches. "It really belongs to him," Overby said, pointing to an ominous figure across the room.

"He told me how to make something like this happen. 'Go home after practice every day and dream about it,' he said 'It'll happen.'"

The man's name was Bobby Bowden

It was 7 P.M. the night of the big game, mighty Oklahoma versus up and surging FSU. Yes, it was a night to remember especially for Bobby Bowden and his Seminole Tribe.

Perhaps, there was a good bit of irony in that fact that FSU would be playing here on this New Years night. For playing the Sooners will complete a full cycle which turned the Seminoles from a laughing matter in 1976 into a serious contender for a national championship.

It all began four seasons ago on a warm September day in Norman, Oklahoma when FSU's first-year Seminole coach, Bobby Bowden took the biggest gamble of his coaching career. The Seminoles prior to their Oklahoma invasion had begun the season with two terrible showings: a 21-12 opening defeat to lowly Memphis State and an embarrassing 47-0 dubbing at the hands of down-state rival, Miami.

"We had to do something," Bowden recalled. "We were playing a tremendous Oklahoma team and I had to shake up my squad. It was a gamble, but I had to take it."

So Bowden gave the wheel a giant spin and made sure it landed on all freshmen members. Seven upperclassmen were benched that immortal day in FSU history and first-year players, receiver Kurt Unglaub, offensive lineman Mike Good, placekicker Dave Cappelen, receiver Jackie Flowers, fullback Mark Lyles, defensive end Scott Warren and defensive tackle Walter Carter received their initial starting assignments.

After 20 minutes of play the Seminoles had a 9-3 lead and although Oklahoma managed to win 24-9, the game gave FSU some hope. And it gave Bowden the knowledge that they could win with youth—and win big.

Since that day in Norman, the Seminoles have compiled a remarkable 34-8 record and more recently a 14-game winning streak.

"That game was definitely the starting point of our team," Bowden now says. "It was the beginning. Now we get a chance to play Oklahoma again on a different ground. It is ironic that those seven freshmen are now seniors and they'll get one more chance at Oklahoma.

Only Unglaub, who was redshirted this season, would not be in the starting lineup this time around. The rest provided the nucleus for this season's nationally-ranked 11-0 team.

"Those seniors are probably the key," Bowden said. "I know we have a strong junior class, but our seniors have gone through the most. They've seen this thing turn around."

And to a man, they surely remember that day in Oklahoma when the ball finally started to roll in their direction.

"I remember those butterflies in my stomach," Carter said. "Boy was I nervous. In high school you dream about playing Oklahoma and there I was, starting against them. I remember having to line up against a guy 6-foot-9, 290 pounds.

John Bridgers (right) and Bowden, accept proclamation from Florida Governor Askew (left) after 1977 successful season.

That was terrifying. As time goes by it seems really weird that I'm ending my career against the same team I started it against. But it's like night and day now.

"Before, we just hoped we could win. Now we know we can win."

The biggest difference now for the Seminoles is confidence.

"We didn't have anything to lose back then," said Scott Warren. "Now we have a lot to lose. I remember those 72,000 screaming fans in Norman. We were an easy game on their schedule then. Now we're a tough game. We're all so much more confident now. Four years ago is a very long time for the FSU football program."

Good, a 6-2, 245-pound offensive guard, was about the same size four years ago, but says the entire FSU team has grown quite a bit since then.

"We've grown in ability and we've grown in confidence," he says. "That game gave us seniors something to remember. Oklahoma didn't think we were much. In fact, we were wondering if they would blow us out of the stadium. After we got that early lead they got serious real quick. Man, I've never seen so many big players in my life.

"We really didn't deserve much back then, but now we deserve a lot. Before, we were happy to just stay close. Now staying close won't be enough. We want to win this one."

And added Unglaub, "the coaches always said we could compete against anybody and that game proved it."

The Seminoles know this year's Oklahoma team is probably better than the 1976 team. However, while they were 30-point underdogs four years ago, they'll be touchdown underdogs this time.

"Maybe they'll take us lightly," Bowden revealed. "But I don't think so. Once you get to a big bowl, you're talking about the cream of the crop. I think they realize that. I think they know we're good."

But if they don't know it, there are seven seniors on this year's team who will gladly remind them.

"We all remember the 1976 game," Warren said. "We just never thought we'd get a chance to even the score. Now we have that chance and we're determined not to let it get away. We've got something to prove to ourselves."

* * *

It was a story not to be forgotten in Gatorland for a long, long time. It all unfolded on the artificial turf in a beserk University of Florida Stadium with one second on a glaring clock in the sky and television cameramen trembling uncontrollably around the FSU bench.

Admist this maddened scene were 1,000 gallons of adrenalin, loose in the air, spread in a cloud all the way to the Georgia line. And over across the field, the Gator coaching staff was pacing and cringing and prancing and yelping and moaning. Yes, they do that in the SEC. But how long has it been since they've done it in Gainesville?

Well, looking back the previous two seasons to 1977, the Gators have had it mighty tough with their sibling cross-state kin, the Seminoles of Florida State. Such attempts have all

The scoreboard says it all.

proven futile as the Gators have come up short each time in losing to *Bowden and Co.*

And in 1979 the Seminoles proved their point again as they responded to pressure in championship form by breaking out of a 10-10 tie early in the fourth quarter and completed a perfect 11-0 season with a 27-16 victory over their bitter rivals at Florida Field before a sell-out crowd of 58,263 and a national television audience that probably wondered why it was watching a winless team on November 23.

"I told our team before the game that they were going to be in for the fight of their lives," Bowden said. "It's hard to believe that I was serious. After all, Florida was 0-8-1 and coming off 33-10 and 31-3 beatings by Georgia and Kentucky.

"But by the third quarter, the Gators began to make a prophet out of me and the message seeped in. Fortunately, our people wanted to win bad enough and in the fourth quarter came back to win."

* * *

Since Bobby Bowden came back to Florida State and turned the Seminole grid program from near shambles to soaring heights, there has often been a profound curiosity to Bowden success. The magical formula well hidden in Bowden's *Winning Cookbook to Success.*

Since his arrival on the Florida State campus in January, 1976, the Birmingham, Ala., native has turned the Seminole grid program from shambles to one of the rising stars on the collegiate scene. After FSU went 4-29 in three previous campaigns under coaches Larry Jones and Darrell Mudra, Bowden has guided the Seminoles to marks of 5-6, 10-2, 8-3 and 11-0.

"The desires of the players to right a wrong they were not happy with is the reason for our winning," says Bowden. "They were not happy with what they were doing previously.

"We also won because of the diligent work of our assistant coaches. Too much of the credit has gone to me when it has been the assistants, trainers, doctors and managers as well as a Florida State administration who have all been part of our success."

If you know Bobby Bowden, that is a typical statement.

Nobody, however, should really be surprised that Bowden has put the Seminole program back on the winning track. Enthusiasm and discipline are key words which exemplify his overall attitude, both on and off the field.

"I believe in discipline and enthusiasm in everything you do in life, and you coach what you believe. If we can be enthusiastic in the little things we do, it will carry over to a winning season.

"But don't get me wrong about discipline. I believe in letting the players know who is boss, and I believe in some sacrifice and devotion. But discipline can only go so far.

"I've always said that if short hair and perfect manners won football games, the Army-Navy game would be played every year for the national championship."

Bowden's coaching philosophy is quite simple.

"I believe in blocking and tackling," he says. "Everything else in this game is secondary; blocking and tackling will cause wins.

"I don't believe in playing without a scoreboard," says Bowden. "I don't feel there is any accomplishment with a tie. I think if one of my teams was playing Notre Dame for the national title and I had the choice of winning or losing or going for the tie, I would go for the win."

National championship was not a term mentioned with a whole lot of frequency at Florida State until Bowden arrived. He explains it cautiously.

"A national championship is the ultimate in coaching, but I must be realistic," says Bowden. "Every year we set new goals with our team. Our first objective is landing a spot in the top 20. Then we want a bowl bid.

"Now after getting past those goals we can begin worrying about the Top 10. We need a consistent winning record so that we can be a legitimate contender each year for national honors."

The 1977 Tangerine Bowl. Bowden and FSU walked away as winners that night against Steve Sloan and Texas Tech.

Bowden, however, is more than just a football coach. He is also a deeply religious individual who, when he's not on the road recruiting, can often be found at a church podium in Tallahassee or one of the surrounding communities on Sunday mornings.

"I don't preach," Bowden says. "I'm not qualified to preach. I like to share my experiences with God, though, especially with young people.

"God is an integral part of my life. I look to God for guidance but firmly believe God helps those who help themselves. Man must help himself, but also seek guidance.

"Coaching, in a way, has many of the same traits as evangelism. You attempt to make your point, relay your beliefs and encourage your audience to take part in all this. Football or religion, it's much the same."

Definitely, there appears to be enormous substance to this man, Robert Cleckler Bowden. The family, the church and the vocation. Yes, Florida State has more than a football coach who can go 11-0 and beat the Gators for three in a row.

Much more.

15

LSU – The Big Game

Slowly a feeling of urgency began to build within the room. Unimportant items had been placed on a bookshelf somewhere along the way last night. Each had donned his "game face;" the mood was quickly becoming serious so each individual had privately made his pact with God and dedicated himself once more to a purpose that this FSU team had spent three months in preparation. Yes, the challenge had been accepted and this afternoon before a national TV audience the much publicized contest would begin. FSU was ready.

It was Friday, October 26, the eve of the biggest game in the eighteenth head coaching year in the football life of Robert Cleckler Bowden. Outside the dorm, Bowden's youthful FSU squad began to board the sleek *Seminole Express* team bus that would carry them to an awaiting chartered jet for their much anticipated flight to Louisiana.

Slowly, the bus began to roll. Sirens and blue flashing lights from a State Trooper escort led the way through a traffic-packed Pensacola Drive. Along the route through town, flashing lights, fancy billboards, honking horns, and proud fans lined the highway to send their team off to battle another great foe—the LSU Tigers. Together the loyal FSU fans proclaimed to this great entourage "Good luck" and "Go 'Noles."

Once aboard the plane, *Ron Simmons and Co.* settled in their seats for a one hour and fifteen minute flight to Baton Rouge.

"It's a battle," the All America nose-guard said. "Football is a man-made war, except that you can't kill, and tomorrow the team that hits the hardest and the longest—they'll be the winners."

Simmons was right. And except for an occasional remark echoing from the back of the plane, the late afternoon flight was quiet. Real quiet! Each player seemed reserved and their expressions reflected their thoughts as they stared out into the distant horizon. Ann Bowden was aboard. She, too, had made these lonely trips before.

And as the sleek Piedmont 737 soared through the upper atmosphere, one could not help but notice the beautiful, yet endless heavens. But after awhile, the plane began to make its descent. Already waiting at the airport was a police escort . . . more sirens, more blue lights. Then they would travel the final leg of the journey to Tiger Stadium for a brief walk around the field and then onward to the Bellemont Motel, the team headquarters for this mid-autumn gridiron clash.

The evening itinerary revealed that the squad would have a brief snack and a final briefing session with Bowden . . . "lights out" would be at eleven. Suddenly, the young men of Florida State began to realize that tomorrow would be a big day—a very big day.

The seventh Saturday in the eighteenth season for Coach Bobby Bowden began like the first, very early in the morning. It was 4:30 A.M. and the skies still had stars in them, when he eased out of bed, pushed the curtain back, and looked to see what October 27, 1979, had brought to Baton Rouge, Louisiana.

He went back to bed but still couldn't sleep, and at 6 A.M. he was up for good, walking softly around the room so that his wife might rest longer. But she, too, was awake, and they waited together as the biggest day of the biggest game in Florida State football was born.

Mark Lyles found "Death Valley"
and T.V. to his liking as he plowed
up LSU's Tiger Stadium turf.

ABC selected Jimmy Jordan to receive the Outstanding Player Award given by Chevrolet on NCAA College Football — Jordan shot down LSU with 312 yard rifle arm.

The customary crowd was out early, too. Mr. DeBord, the equipment man, was in the restaurant drinking his coffee. He was joined by Jack Stanton, the defensive coordinator and they talked about fishing. Within a few minutes, Ann Bowden arrived for breakfast, and, yes, there was a morning paper to be read.

The day was too slow in getting to its feet but Bowden remained at ease. The final game preparations had been completed by 2 AM in his weekly pre-game strategy session with offensive chief, George Henshaw. Now, it was just a matter of waiting until the big moment came.

Had it been this way forever? No, the Bowden of twenty-five years ago had things to prove. But the Bowden who couldn't sleep Saturday morning, who got up early and paced the floor—he's proved them all.

Later, the boys were coming in from their rooms at the motel as the clock headed toward eleven, Saturday of the big game. Don Fauls, the team trainer, stood between the tables with coaches and players standing, heads bowed, for the prayer.

Then they went at it, demolishing steak, eggs, and toast, for Saturday afternoon before the battle required a lot of energy. Yes, big Ron Simmons was right.

For the regimen this day was similar to the festive pre- battle activities of the knights of King Arthur. And the meal of steak and eggs which was set before each athlete might be compared to the massive feasts once reserved for the brave and gallant. And the respective teams symbolize the warriors who would participate in such a contest: definitely a story straight from the pages of Malory's *Morte d'Arthur*. However, for the time being, this group of eager-faced young men enjoyed a few final minutes of fellowship before the biggest game in their young lives—FLORIDA STATE - LSU.

Slowly a feeling of urgency began to build within the room. Unimportant items had been placed on a shelf somewhere along the way last night. Each had donned his "game face"; the mood was quickly becoming serious so each individual had privately made his pact with God and dedicated himself once more to a purpose that this FSU team had spent three months in preparation. Yes, the challenge had been accepted and this afternoon before a national TV audience the much publicized contest would begin. FSU was ready.

Ah, the football fates were shuffling in a most peculiar way to develop the "comeback team" of gridiron history.

And at this eleventh hour, before the heat of battle, Bobby Bowden the great coach who would lead their charge, began to survey his troops. Inside, he searched for the little things that could help make the difference, help his team win.

Yes, the diamond tip of Bowden's greatness as a coach would rest on the field today. For he could most consistently get his team up, and conversely, he could sense that "coming down day" and do something adequate to meet it.

Usually, he does something in advance. And sensing that his team would need that inspirational boost for LSU, Bowden solved the problem brilliantly by throwing away his famed tandem passing game and opting instead for the aerial specialist Jimmy Jordan to captian the attack. In doing so, he affected football history.

Finally, when the meal was finished, head Coach Bowden stood, and as he did, chairs began to scrape. Soon, the moment became still, and the men of Florida State came to attention.

"There are several reminders," he said. Bowden's voice was low, a teacher reviewing his lesson, matter-of-factly, reasonably. It preached, "If they do this . . . if we do that . . . kickoffs, punts, returns, defenses, offenses." And his audience gave undivided attention.

"If we get a bad break," he shrugged, "so what? Then we'll get a good one. If we get behind, that doesn't change things. Just do what you're capable of doing and MAKE SOMETHING HAPPEN."

Then the gentlemenly coach said, "No matter what happens on the field today, I want you to have fun when you're in there—enjoy yourselves. If you get knocked down, GET UP. I know you're ready to play—just keep your pride and confidence on the field and PLAY WITH CLASS. But also remember that those sixty minutes on the field may help determine the rest of your life."

And before closing, he added, "Have courage out there today . . . play with ENTHUSIASM."

At noon the buses lined up and the escort began to form. Departure to the battlefield, massive Tiger Stadium and 78,000 screaming fans was scheduled at 12:15 P.M.

The *Garnet and Gold Brigade* departed their rooms to join the entourage. Then, two buses, five trooper cars, and at least a half-dozen others on motorcycles swung into line, leading the way through the traffic thickening with countless thousands of anxious Cajuns on route to the mid-afternoon war-party. U.S. 61 was congested, but the screaming sirens and familiar blue lights quickly cleared a path.

On the bus, there was silence. Bowden, the coach, sat contently, front seat on the right. The players voices were muted and the team continued through downtown Baton Rouge, as the traffic began to halt. The State Troopers, however, were ready. And they quickly guided the team across the median, up the other side of the highway and the buses proceeded on their journey.

Motorists began pulling off to the side of the road and emptied their cars, and crowds lined the highway as the team journeyed their destined route.

"Hey, FSU!" one man yelled.

"That's the football team!" said a youngster perched upon his father's shoulders.

Everywhere, people began yelling as the undefeated 5th-ranked Florida State football entourage made its way through traffic. FSU fans and disbelieving Cajuns were crazy. They saluted the Seminoles with shakers and danced on top of their cars. Several of them were even wearing war-paint and shouting their favorite war-cry: "Go, 'Noles!"

Reaching the LSU campus, additional police motorcycles joined the escort. And in minutes the upper deck of Tiger Stadium appeared in the distance. Up-front, Coach Bowden could be seen glancing at his watch and nervously folding and unfolding the personnel chart in his left hand. This was

Few teams could penetrate the FSU defense in 1979.

the kind of nervousness that had kept him pacing the sidelines on many autumn afternoons—the kind that had built
great men and winning teams.

Before them stood the massive stadium, and quickly the
buses swung into the parking lot and roared toward the team
gate, past all the up-raised, happy, curious faces. A man outside spotted the procession and knew who was there.

"Yay, yay, FSU!" he yelled. And now "Go 'Noles!" . . . "go
get 'em, men!" as hundreds of others joined.

Then the players began filing off, one by one. As usual,
Bowden led the way—through the dressing room, grabbing a
program, and out onto the field for a brief walk around.

As the group continued its walk the FSU cheering section
saw Bowden and his team and responded. "Hey, Coach
Bowden! Go get 'em!"

Slowly around the field—and the FSU Fighting Chiefs
Band struck up the fight song and the student body saluted
the squad.

"Into the dressing room," Bowden ordered. And the team began to dress. The helmets, the gold silk pants with garnet stripes, the pads, and finally the garnet jerseys, all reminiscent of a medieval arming scene where the knights prepare for battle by donning their suits of armor.

Bowden looked at his squad fondly, then turned and studied the vast stadium filling fast with the greatest throng ever gathered for a FSU football game—78,000 fans. And most of them were hostile.

It was 2:45 P.M. on the seventh Saturday in the eighteenth head coaching year in the football life of Bobby Bowden.

Yet, he went to his task with the enthusiasm and zeal of a younger coach, and such tensions that might clutch him were hidden inside, deep, not to be seen or told. For Bowden's system is good, very good.

Finally at 3:07 P.M., poker-faced Bobby Bowden and his FSU squad went toward another autumn date with destiny, another Saturday grown tremendous.

"Good luck" a man shouted. "Go get 'em!"

"Thank you," Bowden replied, "We'll give it our best shot."

16

T.V. Star

Each Sunday is the same; it's Saturday nights, however, that cause the excitement. The night before this day Bowden had watched, amazed, as his mighty Seminoles had totally dominated always powerful LSU 24-19, with an aerial game like none unleashed before in Tiger Stadium.

Pick a Sunday, any Sunday, from early September onward to the end of November. They're all the same. The alarm sounds at 4:20 A.M. and a lone light clicks on at the home of Florida State head coach, Bobby Bowden.

Outside, the plush Killearn Country Club Estates neighborhood is still blanketed with darkness and dew. Bowden, however, goes about his customary routine of preparing for another big game in the life of FSU football.

Slowly, morning comes to life in Tallahassee; yet there is no one awake for miles except the groggy football coach. Even across town, on campus, parties have ended and the diehards are lapsing into sleep.

Another college football Saturday has come and gone and it is now Bowden's job—red eyes and all—to tell a state-wide television audience what happened to the garnet and gold clad Seminoles and why.

The lonely trek 15 miles up toward Thomasville, Ga. and television station WCTV is a fast paced trip. It is there the program is taped and quickly taken to Jacksonville to be sent to stations in Florida and South Georgia.

When he's not working, eating, or playing golf, Bowden has been known to take cat naps in cars, on the sofa in his office, or in this photo, on a plane ride to 1973 West Virginia-Miami game.

Each Sunday is the same; it's Saturday nights, however, that cause the excitement. The night before this day Bowden had watched, amazed, as his mighty Seminoles had totally dominated always powerful LSU 24-19, with an aerial game like none unleashed before in Tiger Stadium.

And on this 20th morning, October, 1979, Bobby Bowden arrives at the WCTV studio a very happy man. He has made his mark.

Greeted by audio man, Melvin Blank, Bowden asks, "The film here yet?"

"No sir, not yet," replies Blank.

In the meantime he hands Bowden a copy of Saturday's college scores and FSU stats from the previous day's contest.

A few minutes later Blank reports, "There's not much time, Coach."

"Good," replies Bowden. "That's the way I like it. Don't like thinking about it too much."

"Coach, the film just arrived," says director Eliot Toole. "Why don't you step in this other office so you can review it."

Bowden watches as Toole explains the details.

"We always have problems," he says. "Time is the biggest. Getting the film here and then getting it to Jacksonville so they can run it down the network lines at 10 a.m. is the biggest. One of the stations airs it live so it has got to be there.

"We used to try to fly it to Jacksonville but with the weather we were taking a 50-50 chance, so now we're going to drive it there. It takes 2½ hours, but we're assured of making it."

There has never been a retake of the show; any blatant mistakes hit the cutting room floor by way of Toole's scissors.

Blank interrupts Bowden's study of the statistics. "We're about ready."

"Oh jeez," Bowden says. "I haven't thought about any dad-burn introduction yet. I've gotta get something to say."

Two chairs and a coffee table provide the studio stage. Two Styrofoam, construction paper-covered pillars with Seminole logos frame Bowden. It looks cheap to the eye, but television does wonders for it.

"Morning, Coach," says cameraman Ron Rumsey. "Morning, boy," replies Bowden. "You survive last night all right?"

Bowden pauses and turns to a friend. "What was Sain's first name anyway?"

"The baseball player?"

"Yeah, the baseball player. He used to pitch with Warren Spahn on the Milwaukee Braves when they won the pennant. 'Spahn and Sain and pray for rain.'"

"Johnny," is the answer.

"That's it. Johnny Sain and Warren Spahn."

"Stand by, Coach," warns Rumsey as background music

begins to play and a narrator starts the introduction.

Bowden folds his hands and begins.

"Back in the '50s the Milwaukee Braves baseball team had a pitching combination it relied on that won it the pennant. Spahn and Sain and pray for rain, they used to say, because if one wasn't hot, the other was.

"Well, here at Florida State we've got Jimmy Jordan and Wally Woodham and thank goodness for that against LSU. We'll be back in one minute to take a look at yesterday's highlights."

The audio of a commercial comes in and Bowden rubs his eyes, yawns again and collects his thoughts. The camera is ready for him again.

"Here at Florida State we're gonna find a way to make it interesting," he says. "We haven't had anybody try to turn in their ticket yet."

The film moves through the highlights. Bowden ad-libs every series, mentioning as many players as he can on each play. And their hometown. The people there like to hear it and it's good for recruiting.

"In on that tackle was Paul Piurowski from Sarasota," he says. "Paul's mother and girlfriend went over to see the game and it sure was good to see them."

Bowden mentions managers, coaches, cheerleaders, fans and Sgt. Billy Smith, the team's security chief. He gets everybody into the act because everybody associated with the program is family.

The plays run, one after another, on into the morning until the miraculous touchdown reception by senior Jackie Flowers. The play runs four times from four different angles.

"Jackie, oh my goodness, Merriwell," says Bowden, losing himself in the heroic finishes of Frank Merriwell. "Whatever the heck your name is.

"Jackie, I never loved you so much in all my life as I did then. Fourth and 22 . . . I could have hugged you."

Bowden comes back after a commercial to plug next week's game with tough Cincinnati.

"Is it OK?" he asks Toole in the booth.

Bowden gets the thumbs up and begins the trip back to Tallahassee. There are only two other cars on the highway and they pull boats. Killearn is still asleep as the headlights cut through the damp morning air. It's still dark, but the upper regions of the eastern sky are beginning to glow with the first light of day.

"Got to get some sleep," says Bowden, pulling in his driveway. "Got to meet some recruits who are coming by at 8:30 on their way back to Georgia. And then I have to meet some more at the field house at 10. And then church and then meetings all day. Sundays are always rough for a coach."

Especially between 4 and 5 a.m.

17

Promises of Gold

Success, however, is also recognized instantly. And other schools began to measure FSU's newly found success as a chance to play a tempting card, to lure away, Bowden, their Seminole Savior. Most noted of all was heavyweight LSU. For the Cajuns were prepared to thrust deep into their bayou billfold to seek his services.

It was the morning of November 5, 1979, the day that Bobby Bowden and Florida State University were to trade their promises of gold. The day that the Seminoles were to stand-up and be counted in front of college football's elite. The day that FSU finally proclaimed—*We Believe.*

Life has changed down in Tallahassee, for these are now happy days, when football has become tops, and all of the trimmings and hoopla are new, bright and exciting for FSU fans who have waited a long, long time for national recognition of their now mighty Seminoles. And the fans must only look over their shoulders at those humble beginnings of 1947 to see that FSU football has traveled a lengthy path, real quick-like, from its early days as the Florida State College for Women.

It all began in 1946 when a proud post-war America was returning to life once again. Suddenly, women's colleges everywhere were becoming coeducational to accommodate the rapid influx of returning veterans. And it was because of that need that Florida State University was formed. Shortly thereafter, in 1947, the Seminoles fielded their first football team, which turned-in five straight losing efforts against a similar number of smaller college teams.

But things turned around rather quickly, as the Seminoles won seven of eight games in 1948, nine of 10 in 1949, and emerged unbeaten in 1950. In 1951, FSU began its move to the bigger league when it played its first major college

The dynamic duo, Jimmy Jordan, and Wally Woodham, together scout the opposition from the side line.

"Behind, 21-7, in the 3rd quarter against Cincinnati, we had a lot to talk about."

opponent—the University of Miami. And quickly the following season other big league opponents, such as N.C. State, Georgia Tech, and Southern Mississippi, were added to the schedule.

In the meantime, cross-state rival, the University of Florida, refused to recognize the upstart Seminoles.

It was not until 1958, after years of much debate and considerable political pressure in the state legislature, that the Florida Gators were forced to break a long-standing tradition and show-up for a gridiron contest with youthful FSU. And

"When little Kurt Unglaub has the ball, sometimes they catch him, sometimes they don't."

ever since that date it has become an annual affair, although in the eyes of many Florida graduates, Florida State has always been, and always will be, considered second rate.

Slowly, as the years passed, the Seminole program began to grow. Along the way, FSU had a succession of coaches and a modicum of success, playing in nine minor bowl games. And there were some scintillating moments, like the rout of Oklahoma in 1964 Gator Bowl and the game-tying effort against top-ranked Alabama in 1967. Some outstanding individuals soon left their mark at Florida State, including such fine receivers as Fred Biletnikoff and Ron Sellers, and talented quarterbacks like Ken Hammond and Gary Huff. Passing, you see, has been and still is, the mark of Seminole football.

But a losing aura gradually permeated the strength of the Seminoles until they ebbed all the way to a 20-game losing streak in 1973 and 74. During that time reports surfaced that then-coach Larry Jones' practice tactics included chicken-wire cages, which enclosed FSU players and subjected them to unwarranted punishment. After that, came the liberal leadership of Darrell Mudra. His was supposed to have been a different approach to a different breed of people and figured to be conducive to the changing athlete. But the looseness and informality failed to produce a winner.

Other Florida State sports' programs were suffering as well. Even the school president cried—"Raise some support or the program will fold." And responding to the call in the mid-seventies, the Seminole Boosters Club emerged and quickly raised $250,000.

FSU football, however, was aimless. Since Mudra failed to provide the type of leadership that they expected, the Boosters once again stepped forward and bought-off his contract just as they previously had done with Larry Jones. But two losing efforts and $110,000 paid out to ex-coaches were enough to kindle a fire under dissatisfied FSU folks to stand-up and demand "enough of this stuff!"

It was at this moment that Bobby Bowden stepped forward from a winning, and proven, program at West Virginia and accepted the monumental undertaking of rebuilding the football fortunes at deeply troubled Florida State.

But Bobby Bowden, the little guy with guts like a John Wayne, knew the winning formula, and he attacked the toughest rebuilding job in all of college football with unwavering pursuit. Armed with a warm smile, a firm handshake, and a personality that wins instant respect, the new head coach set out on a whirlwind schedule of visiting more cities around the state than *Air-Florida* could arrange flights. Yes, Bowden was taking his cause to the people and immediately they became sold on the New Regime at Florida State, and began rallying together to eliminate "that long standing Gator complex" which had infiltrated the minds and souls of nearly every Floridian.

And things changed. Hard work and good recruiting saw to that. After three-and-one-half years and 31 wins, Bobby Bowden's program has finally reached the upper echelon of college football powers. Now, the Seminoles have become one of the big boys, ranked there with the Alabama's, the Ohio State's, the USC's, and the Oklahoma's.

Success, however, is also recognized instantly. And other schools began to measure FSU's newly found success as a chance to play a tempting card, to lure away Bowden, the Seminole Savior. Most noted of all was heavyweight LSU. The Cajuns were prepared to thrust deep into their bayou billfold to obtain his services. As a matter of fact, Bowden became their top choice to replace highly successful, 18-year veteran Charlie McClendon, the lame duck coach who was being ousted because he couldn't beat the legendary Paul Bryant.

Eventually, other top flight coaches were mentioned for the LSU job—Arkansas' Lou Holtz; Ara Parseghin, the former Notre Dame great; and Bo Rein from N.C. State. But head and shoulders above them all was Bowden. He was the *top* choice.

Florida State, in the meantime, was beginning to understand the X's and O's of the importance of big-time football,

Defensive end, Scott Warren, was one of seven freshmen in 1976 to later lead the Seminoles to glory in 1979.

especially with that number 31 that Bowden had listed in the win column. Without a doubt, FSU's hand was forced.

Quickly, Seminole Boosters and school president, Dr. Bernie Sliger huddled together to plan their strategy. And according to one influential supporter who was involved with the LSU-Florida State power plan, "There was just no way that we were gonna allow another school to ride in on our turf with a raiding party to steal our coach."

Banding together, the group began to build the necessary financial strength to save their flourishing football program. And on Monday, November 5th, they offered Bowden a lavish deal that was intended to provide security for both Bowden and the program. And it was a beauty of a pact, the kind that attempts to discourage controversies like the one encountered by Chuck Fairbanks, the University of Colorado, and the New England Patriots in 1978.

So that afternoon at the magic hour of 4:30 P.M., Bowden stepped forward from the surrounding onlookers and quickly laid to rest any doubts or suspicions about who would be head coach at Florida State.

He said, "I want to be the head coach at Florida State from now on because we're gonna build tradition into this program just like they've done at other tradition football teams. I love the fans, the state of Florida and the enthusiasm that everyone has around here. Hopefully, this thing is gonna last forever."

And with the signing of the new contract, Bowden became one of the nation's highest paid coaches, bumping him into the big dollar league with Chuck Fairbanks of Colorado, Paul "Bear" Bryant of Alabama, Joe Paterno of Penn State, Lou Holtz of Arkansas, Johnny Majors of Tennessee, and Barry Switzer of Oklahoma.

The terms included in the contract specifically called for: (1) a $52,000 salary, (2) a $55,000 television guarantee, (3) a $10,000 expense account, (4) an $11,000 insurance annuity, plus, (5) a couple of cars and various other investments and fringe benefits.

The shiny new Bowden-FSU contract had some intriguing clauses, too. Especially the one the Boosters had inserted to ward off the LSU's, the North Carolina's, the Missouri's and the SMU's who had sought Bowden's services in the recent past. It called for automatic renewal of the contract each December 1, for five more years unless either Bowden or FSU had other ideas.

The exhaustive negotiations were finished. The merger had become rock solid; FSU was committed to furnish Bowden with an annual salary of $128,000 for winning football games and Bowden was committed to FSU, no matter how green the pasture looked on the other side of the fence—unless, of course, a big college strongboy such as an Alabama or a Notre Dame wanted to steal Bowden in 1980, in which case the Crimson Tide or the Fighting Irish would have to reimburse FSU for all five years remaining on his contract—a total of $640,000.

Yet, amidst all of the fame and fortune, Bowden had a key insight to such happenings that truly reveals the character of the man. "I want it this way. The pressure is on me, the head coach, not my staff or the team. And when tomorrow morning comes, we're gonna go back to work and continue to build this program together. We still have big goals to reach."

Pausing for a moment, then continuing, he said, "I hope that it's possible for me to remain at Florida State for a long, long, time."

18

The Man, Bowden

Dear Lord,
  In the battle that goes on for life, I ask for a field that is fair, a chance that is equal with all in strife. The courage to do and to dare.
  If I should win let it be by the code, my faith and my honor held high.
  If I should lose let me stand by the road and cheer as the winner rides by.

  Knute Rockne

It was May 2, 1980, on a beautiful, warm Florida late afternoon in the plush football coaching office that serves gridiron mentor, Bobby Bowden. As usual, the day had been jam packed with meetings, press interviews and visits from FSU fans coming into town for the annual Garnet vs. Gold Spring game to be played the next day before 40,000 enthusiastic Seminole fans and a national television audience.

However, now, as the pre-game festive hoopla had finally settled down for the remainder of the day, Bowden left the comforts of his luxurious office chair and walked over to one of the two windows that looks outward to an ever growing Doak Campbell Stadium.

Glancing from left to right, he envisioned the progress that soon would take place . . . *"A $200,000 scoreboard like they have at LSU—great . . . Another 5,500 seats on the west side of the stadium—one day we'll have Notre Dame and Alabama playing us at home with 72,000 seats . . . Brand*

"At West Virginia, we taught our quarterbacks that if they couldn't stand the heat, then they should get out of the kitchen."

Bobby Bowden's brand of football builds character,
self-discipline and a winning attitude.

IT BEGINS with
BOWDEN!

new television lights and new electrical wiring worth $500,000—ABC is gonna love that . . . All of those people coming to the Spring game tomorrow—boy, I hope this lasts forever at Florida State!"

Then, Bowden returned to his desk, opened one of the file drawers and removed a faded note pad. Reviewing the pages one by one, he carefully studied the notes he had been keeping for twenty-odd years. For these were the little things that motivates the man, Bowden.

And as they poured forth to his special quest, one could not help but understand the importance of this rare moment. For there were the characteristics of this winning coach— Bobby Bowden.

"Good steel must go through the hottest fire.

"The greatest mistake of all is to continue 'practicing a mistake.'

" 'Trust in the Lord with all thy heart . . . and He will direct thy path.' (Proverbs 3:5-6)

"If you can't stand the heat, then get out of the kitchen.

"TEAM RIGHTS SUPERCEDE INDIVIDUAL RIGHTS.

"Don't lose your GUTS; if you believe in your plan, carry it out regardless.

"Winston Churchhill, Thomas Edison, Blanton Collier, Paul Brown, Vince Lombardi, and Ben Franklin *all* made mistakes, but they shook them off to become very successful. At certain times, however, they were all downright losers.

"Everybody makes mistakes, even Coach Bryant. In 1965 against Tennessee with a 7-7 tie, his team had made a mistake that cost them the game when Bryant sent in a play which he thought would be a good 3rd and 7 play. Unfortunately, Bryant had gotten confused. It was 4th down and Alabama had to settle for a 7-7 tie.

"Face life's issues . . . now.

" 'Depend upon the Lord and He will grant your heart's desire.' (Psalm 37:4)

"The Peach Bowl in 1972 taught me to never get relaxed before a big game. We ended up losing 49-13 to N.C. State. After that humiliating defeat, I'll never let my guard down.

"It is better to have faith in a cause that will ultimately succeed than to succeed in a cause that will ultimately fail.

"If a dog won't do what you teach him to do . . . then teach him to do what he can do.

Responsibility without *authority* will result in failure.

" 'He that hath knowledge spareth his words . . . Even a fool, when he holdeth his peace, is counted wise.' (Proverbs 17:27-28)

"Be confident in this very thing that God, who has begun a work in you, will complete it.' (Phillippians 1:6)

"When two partners always agree, then one of them is not necessary.

"If you were being tried for being a Christian, would they have enough evidence to convict you.

A player who wants long hair is an individual. You can't win with individuals.

"GOD DON'T SPONSOR NO FLUNKIES' . . . if you are one of His, He'll want you to succeed.

"We ask for *strength* and God gives us difficulties that makes us strong. We pray for *wisdom* and God sends us problems, the solution of which develops wisdom. We plead for *prosperity* and God gives us brains and brawn to work. We pray for *courage* and God gives us dangers to overcome. We ask for favors . . . God gives us opportunities. This is the answer.

"O Lord, help my words to be gracious and tender today, for tomorrow I may have to eat them.

" 'Have I not commanded thee? Be strong and of good courage. Be not afraid, neither be thou dismayed; for the Lord thy God is with thee withersoever thou goest.'

"Christ was tough minded but tender hearted.

"Why worry . . . when you can pray.

"The only thing to fear is fear itself.

" 'I run straight to the goal with purpose in every step. I fight to win.' " (I Corinthians 9:26)

19

The Perfect Season

With a perspiring 2:40 to play in the final quarter, Woodham began the "do-or-die" drive, calling first on fullback, Lyles, who responded by bringing the Seminoles 31-yards closer. Next, Woodham sent Mark Whiting outside as he bumped and scrambled his way for the final distance, thus preserving the win streak.

It was 1973, the year that Florida State football went 0 and 11 and was near the brink of extinction. Miraculously, the program managed to struggle along.

Then in 1976, Bobby Bowden arrived in Tallahassee and quickly began to convince the Seminoles that they could be *winners*. Armed with a steel will to succeed, Bowden turned the program around, so much so, that in 1979, Florida State did not lose a game and finished the regular season ranked #4 in the nation. Finally, the once down-trodden Seminoles had earned their place among the elite in college football.

The crowning point to this success story, of course, came with an invitation for FSU to play in the much coveted post-season Orange Bowl classic in Miami. Definitely, it was a well deserved reward for an incredible year, one which involved a unique two-quarterback shuffle, a defense that ranked among the ten best in college football, and a series of heart stopping come-backs that preserved Florida State's first undefeated season in major college football.

Yes, the unpredictable rise to 11 and 0 was so suspenseful that it could have provided the plot for one of FSU's former football players, Burt Reynolds', many thrilling movies. 1979—it was definitely a year to remember.

The perfect season, however, had some difficult beginnings. In the opening game of the season against Southern Mississippi with a crowd of 45,000 enthusiastic fans on hand, the Seminoles entered the fourth quarter *trailing 14-3.* It appeared as if defeat was only a matter of time for Bobby Bowden and his hard-fighting crew. But the determined Seminoles would not give up the battle. Somehow there would emerge a pathway to victory.

Finally, the much needed break that Bowden had often preached about came when relief signal caller, Jimmy Jordan, found senior wide receiver, Jackie Flowers, in the endzone for the season's first touchdown. Now the scoreboard in Doak Campbell Stadium read 14-10.

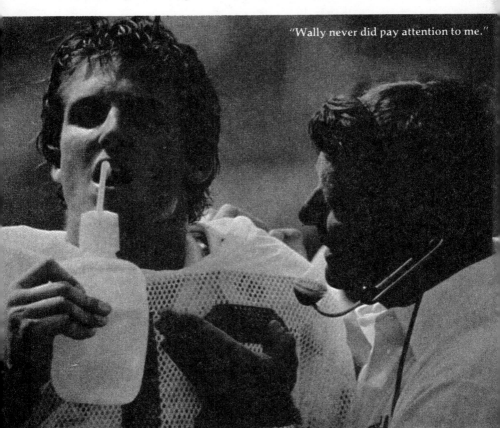

"Wally never did pay attention to me."

"Neither did Jimmy. Maybe that's the reason that we won at FSU."

Minutes later, however, sophomore Gary Henry found the Seminole remedy when he spotted a gapping whole while fielding a punt return and wasted no time in rallying 65 yards for the game-breaking score. The Seminoles were on top, 17-14. But with the final outcome still in question, field general, Jimmy Jordan, wasn't to be denied. He quickly marched the garnet and gold warriors downfield for a final scoring burst, once again hitting wide receiver Jackie Flowers for the game clinching points—the eighth 4th quarter comeback in 24 triumphs for Bowden's FSU teams.

A week later, defense grabbed the headlines for the first time in a long time at Florida State as junior walk-on, Monk Bonasorte, the Seminole's quiet unassuming defensive leader picked off 2 Arizona State aerials. By season's end, young Bonasorte would wind up with eight interceptions, tying a FSU school record, and earning third team All-America honors.

But the Seminole's sizzling defense, which shut down their Pac-Ten visitors without a touchdown, wasn't the only point of interest in Tallahassee that day. Florida State's two quarterback system had become a national attraction and Coach Bowden found himself caught in a very pleasant dilemma with two top quarterbacks in designated starter, Wally Woodham, and relief pitcher, Jimmy Jordan.

A remarkable point to be noted must be the success story behind this dynamic duo, for both Woodham and Jordan had been in a similar role once before, as teammates at Leon High School in Tallahassee. There, young Wally Woodham had set a national passing record only to have it broken the following year by Jordan. And when they ended up on the same team once again at FSU, both Woodham and Jordan vowed to sacrifice their own individual stardom for the good of the Seminoles. Playing together, they knew that they could become *winners*.

On the heels of a 31-3 shelacking of Arizona State, the two senior signal callers continued to take turns piloting the assault against cross-state rival, Miami. But, "Wally Jim Jordham," as one journalist called them, had to share the hero's role that day with a fast developing running attack. Following the excellent blocking of linemen Gil Westly, Mike Good, Ken Lanier, Greg Futch, and Tom Brandon, big fullback Mark Lyles scored a pair of touchdowns. For on the day of this great sunshine shoot-out, the offensive line and the Seminole runners melted together into a perfect partnership. And when Gary Henry, the sophomore speedster from Orlando, unleashed another long punt return, it reduced the visiting Miami Hurricane to nothing more than a gentle breeze.

That day, the Seminoles scored 40 points on their downstate rivals with a solid defense, reliable running, and an awesome air game. Yes, the Florida State Seminoles were now ready for anyone. And during the next two weeks, dreams of a high national ranking and maybe even an undefeated season began to surface.

Against previously unbeaten Virginia Tech, senior running back Greg Ramsey's 16-yard touchdown romp helped FSU cement its first road victory of 1979. But as so often in the past, it was not easy. The clincher finally came on the skillful accuracy of quarterback Jimmy Jordan and the gluefinger hands of Jackie Flowers, as they paced the Seminoles to another touchdown and a narrow 17-10 victory.

The next week, the running of big Mark Lyles sparked the total dominance of the Louisville Cardinals, along with two scoring passes from Wally Woodham.

Throughout those first five victories of 1979, if there was one convincing, yet unexpected key to success, it had to be the menacing play of the Seminole defense. For they were a group of hitters who either took the offense out of the fight, or the fight out of the offense. At Louisville, senior co- captain Scott Warren blocked a punt for a safety and Ed Richardson put his body in front of another Cardinal punt as cornerback, Bobby Butler, chased it down for six points and a touchdown.

The "Seminole Sackers" had become a force that opponents now had to deal with in addition to the offense. And while it was a total *team* defense, its foundation was not difficult to locate. Big noseguard Ron Simmons became the guy who cemented the Seminole defense together as he stayed in the middle holding together the right side with the left. And All-America, Simmons and his teammates rose to the occasion when needed in 1979. The rock hard wall of Arthur Scott, Jeremy Midlin, Mark Macek, Scott Warren and Simmons proved nearly impossible to penetrate, and they hurried passes into the eager awaiting arms of Seminole defensive backs such as Keith Jones, Bobby Butler, Ivory Joe Hunter, Monk Bonasorte, or linebackers Reggie Herring and Paul Piurowski. Devastating defense had indeed found a

In 1979, Bowden's team ran through their opposition with ease.

home at Florida State. And Mississippi State felt the sting of the defense as they became victim number six, 17-6.

The next week, however, the most difficult test of the season lay waiting in Baton Rouge as the Seminoles were to take on LSU in a Tiger's den where many a great team had been devoured. Another highlight to the pressure packed contest was the fact that ABC decided to televise the Cajun-Seminole war party.

As *Bowden and Co.* stepped onto the natural turf at LSU, the gambling gridiron genius decided to break from his past tradition of starting Wally Woodham and instead, opted to call on his relief pitcher, Jimmy Jordan, the strong-armed passer's first start in over a year. But Bowden knew his

Game breaking touchdown run against Miami gave Mark Lyles, 48, and teammates something to celebrate."

players, and in the season's only departure from the two quarterback system, Jordan responded by playing the entire game and rifling three touchdown passes, thus earning the game's MVP for ABC television. Suddenly, the FSU aerial assault had laid seige to Baton Rouge, and the football world began to take notice that the Seminoles were climbing toward the top. And as Jackie Flowers noted in the locker-room after the biggest game in FSU history, "FSU—we're now for real!"

The celebration, unfortunately, was to be short lived as the Seminoles were about to suffer a scare that threatened the foundation of their newly acquired national prominence. In their next game, Cincinnati blasted the Seminoles from every direction. In the fourth quarter, FSU found itself trailing 21-7, and Bowden began to fear that his team's win streak had come to an unexpected end.

But amidst the threats of defeat, Bowden and his players reached down inside to muster new courage within themselves and find the comeback key to victory. And as time was to prove, there were to be many heroes for Florida State on that immortal memorable day.

Senior Mark Lyles began the momentum as he ran, not to be denied the goal line, to score the first points in the long struggle back. Tailback Mark Whiting added some more clutch running when needed, but the key to the comeback was quarterback Wally Woodham; with injured All-America Ron Simmons coming off the bench to single-handedly ignite a defense which was to shut out Cincinnati in the second half, Woodham mixed the offensive plays masterfully.

With a perspiring 2:40 to play in the final quarter, Woodham began the "do-or-die" drive, calling first on fullback, Lyles, who responded by bringing the Seminoles 31-yards closer. Next, Woodham sent Mark Whiting outside, bumping and scrambling his way for the final distance, thus preserving the win streak.

Later Woodham was to comment, "We were faced with adversity, but like a true champion, we pulled together as a team and turned defeat into victory."

Definitely, it was another peak in a season at the summit. And the success of this undefeated FSU football team was beginning to engulf the campus as students began to cheer their efforts and pat them on the back, for jobs well done. In Tallahassee, everyone began to share in this new found national prominence.

The next week, a record-setting Doak Campbell Stadium welcomed South Carolina with much gusto. And on the field, the Seminoles, behind the sure-footed kicking of Davey Cappelen's four field goals and the hard hitting efforts of the stingy FSU defense, limited the Gamecocks and the country's leading rusher, John Rogers, to a single touchdown as sixth ranked FSU went on to win, 27-7.

Then, a bid to play in the Orange Bowl on New Year's night came following a 66-point runaway against Memphis State that saw defensive back, Keith Jones, score a touchdown with a blocked punt and linebacker Paul Piurowski enjoy the thrills of a running back as he intercepted a pass to set up a touchdown. Yet, on offense, Bobby Bowden football was displayed at its finest as 11 different receivers caught passes and all nine touchdowns were scored by different players. Now, the Seminoles were but one game from a perfect season.

But what a game it was to be—the in-state rivalry with the winless Gators of Florida—the game that meant so much to in-state recruiting and allowing oneself to live with honor for another year. On this day after Thanksgiving with a national television audience watching, there was definitely a lot at stake.

In the first two periods the Seminole defense controlled the action. Then, following a Davey Cappelen field goal in the waning moments of the first half, the FSU offense began to flex its muscle. On second-and-six from the Seminole's 33 yard line field general, Jimmy Jordan, passed 25 yards across the middle of the field to tight end Grady King to the Gator 42. Two plays later Jordan again passed to King to set up a first down at the Gator 21. And then on the next play, Jordan passed 21 yards to freshman, Hardis Johnson, with only 11 seconds remaining in the half, to put the Seminoles up, 10-0.

However, in the third quarter the stubborn Gators came back to tie the score 10-10. Not to be denied victory against Florida, the bullish fullback, Mark Lyles from Buffalo, NY, powered his way to a career high of 151 yards to two touchdowns. Finally, after two previous wins over the Gators, the Seminoles now had a lead they weren't about to relinquish. They could taste their long awaited perfect season as years of hard work and total dedication by everyone was about to pay off. And when Mark Lyles embraced the end zone for the second time in the game, the Seminoles had completed the dream of every player, coach, and fan of amateur or professional sport—they had their perfect season.

20

This I Believe

Bowden, however, is more than a figure-head Christian. He addresses church congregations on the average of twice-a-week. "I've always believed in God, the Bible and Jesus Christ, he says. "The talents God's given you should be used for His glory."

Bobby Bowden describes himself as an alcoholic who has never touched a drink. Football is his bourbon, golf his scotch, and eating his six pack of tall boys.

In four years, Bowden has brought the Florida State football program from the ploddings of mediocrity to the unprecedented heights of an undefeated regular season, a No. 4 national ranking and a New Year's night engagement in the Orange Bowl.

In the public eye, Bowden is known as a cunning football strategist, a superb motivator of young men, a corn-pone quipper, and a deeply religious individual.

During his career, he has been hanged in effigy and carried off the field on the shoulders of his players. At times, he talks like Gomer Pyle, but what he says keeps governors and Ph.D.'s spellbound. He's called a hillbilly, yet grew up in the city.

He has his favorites, too. Glenn Miller plays the best tunes, Bear Bryant calls the best plays, and Bob Hope tells the funniest jokes.

But there is more, much more to this 50-year-old ruler of Tallahassee. His close friends have a love for him that super-

Coach Bowden and his lovely wife, Ann, during a summer golf outing.

cedes his coaching fame. To them, Bobby Bowden is a God-loving family man, a live-by-the-rules sort of guy.

Bowden, however, is more than a figurehead Christian. He addresses church congregations on the average of twice-a-week. "I've always believed in God, the Bible, and Jesus Christ," he says. "The talents God's given you should be used for His glory."

Recently, at a Baptist church in Jacksonville he told his youthful audience, "I want to be on God's squad—He's *my* kind of head coach." And when he speaks of his convictions, they flow freely and always lack the distasteful traces of religious overkill.

"I don't feel qualified to preach," he often says. "However, my son, Steve, who is in the Baptist Seminary in Louisville, Kentucky, *is* qualified. He's the preacher in the family."

And when Bowden talks to young people, adults, or a gathering of coaches, his messages are always the simple matter-of-fact testimonies that make you feel proud to be an American.

Yes, there is an aura of goodness about this man.

*   *   *

Bowden, much like the late Will Rogers, is a story teller. He loves to mix his testimonies with an occasional flare of humor. They're always folksy and down-to-earth, the kind of stories that Americans love to hear. The kind that people want to stand-up and applaud upon hearing.

. . . "When I was a youngster, I always had a thrill of going to the Palace Shoe Shop near our house in East Lake, just so that I could see the shoemaker nail those half-inch nails into the shoes and then give them a shine that made 'em look brand new. Today, that same old shoe shop has withstood the effects of modernized America because it's still in the same spot and still operated by the same guy who has operated it for nearly forty years.

"Not long ago, while in Tallahassee, Ann and I were going through an old box of high school clothes when we came upon an old worn-out ticket stub for a pair of shoes that I had evidently taken to the shoe shop nearly 30 years ago and forgotten to pick-up.

"Well, I thought to myself, wouldn't it be fun to go by that old shoe shop and see what's happened to it? Who knows, I just might find my long lost pair of shoes.

"Last summer, that opportunity finally came when I was asked to come back and speak to my old church, Ruhama Baptist, there in East Lake. So I walked down the street *on Saturday afternoon* to visit the Palace Shoe Shop, and sure enough, it was still there. And the same little old shoemaker inside, who had lost all of his hair and had those funny bifocals perched on the end of his nose, was in the back of the shop still mending those shoes.

"So I just walked in the shop, whistling up a tune, acting like I had been in the shop only a few days before to deposit those shoes. And when the old shoemaker walks up to the counter, I handed him the old ticket stub and asked, 'Are they ready?'

"Well, that old shoemaker took the ticket and spent a few moments, studying it very closely and began to form a curious grin. Next, he walks behind the curtain to the back of the shop and all the time I can hear him stirring about, trying to find those missing shoes.

"After awhile, there's nothing but silence until he finally reappears at the front of the store and with a look of a Boy Scout he says, "If you can come back on Thursday, they'll be ready.'

"Who know's maybe when I go back to Birmingham again, he just may have those shoes ready."

Bowden loves tall tales and he is blessed with the rare, but uncanny, ability to sport the face of a riverboat gambler while telling his story. There's just no way you don't believe him.

. . . "Right after our humiliating defeat in the Orange Bowl game this year I tried to escape the press and media by doing some serious hunting for a few days in Perry, Florida, with my good friend, Jim Smith, the Attorney General of Florida.

"Well, Perry is only 50 miles southeast of Tallahassee and, while we were riding down there, I kept telling Jim about this wonderful farm that a FSU man had and what great hunting we're gonna do. Now, Jim is an avid hunter, so when I got to big-talking about all of this hunting, he got to be all smiles.

"That went on for nearly forty miles until we reached this dirt road about 15 miles outside of Perry, which we turned onto. It was a long and dusty affair for 5 or 6 miles until eventually we reached the perimeter of the farm we're going to and sure enough it was every bit as big as beautiful as I had described—wide rolling pastures, plenty of timberland, lakes, and over a thousand head of cattle. Jim was in hog-heaven.

"So I stopped the car at the front fence and told Jim that I was going to see the old man that owned the place and get our keys to the guest house. Jim just nodded his head in agreement.

"And I walked up to the front door, knocked on it and in a minute or two, the farm's landlord answers the door and welcomes me to his farm. Let me tell you, after the Orange Bowl, it was great to find folks who still cared about you.

"The old man, however, had a big problem that had been facing him for weeks and he asked me, 'Hey, Coach, you've got to do me a favor while you're here this week. Ya see, out in the barn I've got this ol' mule that I've had for 25 years, which is awful diseased. He's really sick and I love that ol' mule.'

"So I said, 'Well, what do you want me to do?'

He replied, 'Would you mind killing him for me!'

"I said, 'Sure'

"So I headed back to the car and while I'm walking I got to thinking to myself, 'Wouldn't it be nice to play a trick on ol' Jim.'

"Well, I got me the most disappointing frown on my face that I figured anybody could wear and went back, jumped in the car and slammed the door.

"Wondering what was going on, Jim asked, 'What happened?'

"I said, 'That mean sonuvagun trade-coating Florida Gator lover won't let us go hunting on this land since we lost so bad to Oklahoma in the Orange Bowl.'

"Big Jim Smith quickly replied, 'Heck, Bobby, maybe we oughta get off his land before he gets upset.'

"Now I wasn't gonna leave just yet, not until I had the opportunity to play my prank on Jim so I got my gun and said, 'Jim, you see that mule standing over there?'

"He said, 'Yeah.'

"So I said, 'Well, watch this.' And then I proceeded to shoot my 12-gage shotgun which quickly put that ol' mule out of its misery. Trying to stifle a smile, I looked at Jim Smith and I could see his eyes getting bigger than half-dollars.

"All of a sudden I heard something go 'bam-bam' and I looked over at Jim and he shouted, 'Let's get out of here, I shot two of his cows.'

"Now, Big Jim won't go hunting with me anymore. I think that one experience was enough."

Then, when Bowden loosens his audience and they're sitting on the edge of their seats, he changes the pace and his message becomes more serious; the real story pours forth.

. . . "I'm a firm believer in God and country and Florida State football. And I'm also a firm believer in the great opportunities that God has given to athletes to witness to young people and grown ups all across this country. I know that it is because of this type *leadership*, I became involved in the Fellowship of Christian Athletes.

"It all began in 1947 in Birmingham when an All-American baseball player, Jackie Robinson from Baylor University, came to Ruhama Baptist Church one night to speak. As usual, Ann was singing in the choir and ol' Bobby was sitting at the back of the church (which I still do today.)

"Jackie Robinson made an impact on me that night. And as I sat in the back pew I kept thinking to myself, 'I wish I could do that' because the common denominator for all young men, especially athletes, and maybe for girls because

Bowden and Seminole Baseball Coach Woody Woodward. Both were big time winners in 1977.

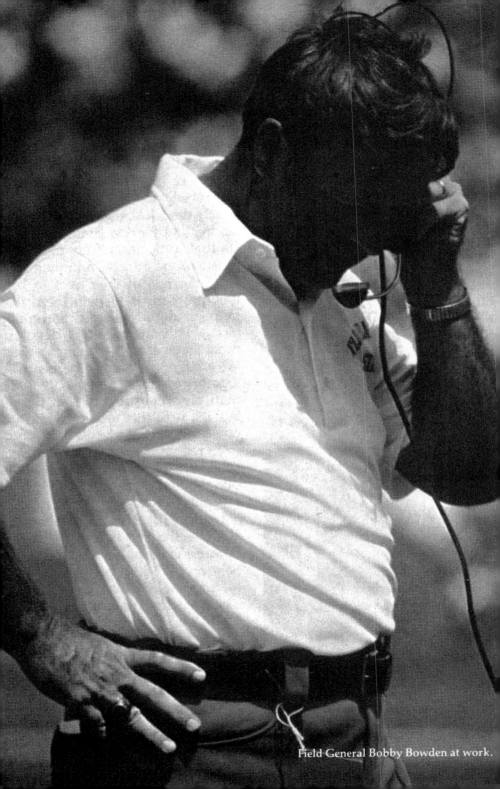

Field General Bobby Bowden at work.

of what the guys are doing, is having that opportunity to stand up in front of everyone and say, 'This I believe.'

"I always love to take an opportunity to share my testimony with young people, especially athletes because I want them to know that, like it or not, they're in the eyes of people. Whether it's one or 100,000. They've got a number on their backs and have been identified. America's big on hero-worship. And I tell them that they're an example whether they want to be or not. I make it clear: 'I don't want to think that somebody's gone bad because of what I've done, do you?'

"I've really been lucky because God lets me support my family, He lets me make a living through coaching the game I love, football, but I still know that the primary responsibility in my life is trying to serve God through football.

"My friend, Bart Starr, the head coach of the Green Bay Packers, once told me a story that his coach, the late Vince Lombardi, told before a season finale with Los Angeles Rams. At the time the Packers were 10 and 1 and divisional champions, while the Rams had won only one game all season. But that 12th game was still there.

"Now, if you've ever coached, its always tough to get a team ready for that last game, especially if you're already the divisional champion and the last game doesn't really count because you've clinched a spot in the play-offs.

"Lombardi, however, was ready. He knew what it would take to get his men up for the game. He told 'em, 'Men, when you go out there today, I want you to give 'em your best. I want you to give up yourself. Because if you don't then you're gonna be cheating . . . Your're gonna be cheating the team, your fellow teammates, the fans sitting up there cheering for you, and your gonna be cheating yourself. But most importantly, your gonna be cheating God, because it was God who gave you that great ability and if you don't do the best that you can, then that is the biggest cheat there is.' That afternoon the Packers won their game.

"Lombardi's philosophy applies to everyone, whether they play football, march in the band or type on a typewriter.

God has given us all a special ability and it's up to us to develop it to our utmost potential because if we don't—we're cheating ourselves and Him.

"Recently, I read in the book of Matthew, 25th chapter verses 14-28, the parable of the talents. And in the modern translation, a talent is a description of a coin. It seems that in the parable Jesus is telling of the three different amounts of talents given to the three servants by their master before he left on a long journey. To one servant the master gave one talent, to another he gave two talents, and to the third, he gave five talents. His only instructions were that he would hold them accountable when he returned.

"In the meantime, the servant who had five talents went out and put his money to work and doubled his investment to ten. The second servant also invested his talents, and soon his two talents had increased to four. But the third servant was different; he never invested his.

"Later, the Master finally returned and when he did, he asked the servants what they had done with their talents.

"One said, 'Master, I had five talents which I used and now here are ten.'

"The Master said, 'You loyal soul, you have done good work and because you have been loyal over a few things, I will make you ruler over many things.'

"Then the Master asked the servant who had two talents what he had done. He replied, 'Sir, I put it to work and increased it to four.' The Master then rewarded him in the same manner as he had rewarded the first servant.

"Finally, the Master asked the servant who had one. And do you know what he did? Probably the same thing as most people do. He said, 'Master, I was afraid that I would loose that talent and I knew that you had worked hard for it, so I took that talent and hid it under a rock where nobody would get it. Here it is back.'

"The Master then got angry at him and took the one talent and gave it to the servant who had ten. Disappointedly, that third servant had wasted the productivity of his talent.

"Personally, that's what life is all about. God may have given each of us one, two, or five talents to use and develop. But if we don't take them and put those talents to work, then we're gonna end up like the third servant—a disappointment.

"And in nearly thirty years of coaching, I've learned a *big* fact of life. It is that God doesn't want your ability. Instead, He wants your *availability*. He needs people who'll say, 'God, here I am. I'm making myself available to you. What do you want me to do?'

"Soon, those opportunities will begin to open-up and God will take you and put your availability and ability to work. And that's when things become worthwhile."

Why, Football?

"What is the reason for spring practice? Have you ever heard of these "anti-football men" say why we shouldn't have it other than the fact that it's too much work for the boys? What do they know about it? Many of them have never engaged in football at all, much less spring practice, and the others fall in line because they think it is all right to be in the swim with other educators. In view of this fact, why should their arguments carry any weight?

When anything is successful, we always hear from some who try to tear it down. There must be something wrong with it they argue or else it couldn't have attained the proportions that it has. Many times the critics are prompted by some form of envy. They do their criticizing from background where they "never walked in the moccasins" of the men or sport, they are criticizing.

At present, so it is with football. It seems to be the custom of a few after every football season, whether or not it is a successful one, to broadcast the cry that the game as it is played today is an unnecessary evil. That in order for our institutions of learning to remain stable, it is necessary that intercollegiate football as it is conducted now, cease.

There is no doubt that Coach Bowden has done a lot to further the game at FSU. He believes in football and all for which it stands. Naturally, when anyone casts a slur at it, he is the first to upset their argument and defend the game he loves. He has done more in its defense than anyone could imagine that any one individual could do.

"When the cry of overemphasis comes up", Bowden suggests, "I always ask myself; has anyone ever defined overemphasis? I am always ready to listen to any arguments that they have, and to reason logically with them, but they only want to bring out the negatives and eliminate the positives.

"Last year, thru the success of our team, our athletic department was able to give our president over $100,000 for academic purposes.

"One would imagine that the game of football has reached such vast proportions that it is entirely out of line with the working of the institutions. In reality, outside of a few inventions and some new ideas, intercollegiate football, as it is played today is not one iota different than it was fifty years ago when Rockne ruled the game. It may seem so because the big crowds of earlier days were ten or fifteen thousand people and now we have anywhere from fifty to a hundred thousand crowding into the stadium. But why do they blame football for these extra people who want to see it played? Isn't this making new friends for the University? Isn't it affording them an opportunity to become more closely associated with it? I believe that it is the idea of the authorities of the American colleges to have as many friends as possible.

"I'm inclined to believe there are too many reformers in the American public. The biggest task that the government has today is to reform the reformers. These people infer that anybody either indirectly or directly interested in football is more or less crazy and unable to see the light because his eyes are blurred with floating specks of pigskin. I'm not inclined to believe that there are over two hundred and thirty million lunatics in this country.

"Let me single out the arguments of some reformers. Their first kick was against spring practice. They said it should be abolished because it extracted too much of a boy's time. If a thorough study was made of it, it will be seen that it does not take up nearly as much time as that of tennis, track, or basketball. The tennis team, for instance, has their fall outdoor practice then in winter time they go indoors followed by a long, strenuous outdoor season which lasts all spring. The foundation of track is laid in the fall in cross country work. After that comes the indoor season which lasts until late March. Then comes the outdoor season which always goes right on into June. Basketball practice begins in the middle of October and goes right through until the middle of March.

"I know that our University heartily endorses all of these sports and maintains that they are fine for the individual, and I use them merely as examples. Each one, however, takes up much more time than does football practice, but their function is still necessary in our society today. If a guy who chooses to play football then also desires to participate in a spring sport, he is allowed to do so. I believe our boys are sent to school primarily to get an education, and the responsibility of their care is placed on my shoulders alone, not on those of other school authorities. For when others are in charge, they can look out for the boys when they are in their classrooms, or when they are in their rooms at night. But there is always the difficult time of the recreation period where the boy might stray.

"Isn't it better to have a group of boys working off their excess energy, which has generated in their systems during the hours of classroom work, on the football fields under capable instruction in organized athletics than it is to have these same young men dashing around in automobiles, loafing on the street corners, poolrooms or the drug stores. In this form of recreation they can easily get in trouble. Then the parents will come back to the authorities with "Why didn't you look after my boy and take care of him?" What our coaching staff at Florida State will try to do is to develop these boys so that their physical triumphs can go hand in hand with their mental achievements in the classroom and believe me—when they go to bed at night, they're going to be so tired that they don't have to stay up half the night thinking up some devilish trick to keep them occupied!

"If a boy wants to come out for spring football, do these reformers want him to be stopped? At Florida State, we have practically every spring sport on our program and yet when the call is put out for football, there is usually a turnout of about fifty boys who come out on their own and are issued equipment. Does that look as though the boys don't enjoy it? This is the condition at our place and I'm speaking only of FSU. I don't know what conditions are at other colleges so it's not for me to say what they should do. Let their own athletics' heads settle their own problems. But I would like to have some of these "anti-football men" talk to any of our football men and find out whether or not spring practice is a bore to them.

"Getting more heated in the argument, let me continue. If the coaches can't make the practice sessions interesting and entertaining for our boys, then they had better get out of the coaching profession. The trouble with so many coaches in the past has been that their work has been more or less tiresome to themselves and this reaction naturally was conveyed to the boys. If the head of a big business always found himself lazy and grumpy, naturally the organization would suffer and turn out to be lazy and grumpy too. I'm sold in my own mind on the fact that spring practice is good for a boy and we're going to have it as long as the fellows want it. Thank God, we have the type of boy at Florida State who prefers physical activity to lounging on street corners.

"What is the reason for spring practice? Have you ever heard of these 'anti-football men' say why we shouldn't have it other than the fact that it's too much work for the boys? What do they know about it? Many of them have never engaged in football at all, much less spring practice, and the others fall in line because they think it is all right to be in the swim with other educators. In view of this fact, why should their arguments carry any weight?

Enthusiasm has been the trademark of FSU's success story.

"At Florida State I believe that we have spring football so that the coaches can better equip the boys with the fundamentals of the game. There is not much time for this in the actual football season because the coaches have to worry more about the condition of the boys, their timing, and the defense they hope to employ to stop their opponents. At Florida State we get our ground work in the spring, where the staff can go into any and every minor detail without fear of losing any time. Then it is not necessary to give hasty instruction. I think it should be the idea of anybody entering into any sort of contest, whether it is business, a debate, or athletics, to have as good a knowledge of what he is trying to do as possible.

"I, as one who advocates the spring practice, want to do justice to a boy. When he goes into the game in the fall, he is going to be that much better. He is going to be able to take care of himself, to meet competition as it comes up in front of him. His reactions to emergencies are going to be quicker. He will coordinate more smoothly. All in all, he will do a much better job. The manager of a boxer doesn't send his fighter into a championship match without the necessary preliminary training, does he? Doesn't the president of a university demand that his faculty members have a Master's degree before they can be called 'professors?' That's preparation, isn't it? Well, that's what our staff is trying to do.

"Pretty soon, if this wrangling gets any louder, spring practice will jump from the status of a 'bone of contention' to a criminal offense. Thirty days in the workhouse will be the penalty for any boy caught throwing a football between the first of January and the first of June. Maybe the word 'practice' is what annoys them. If so, then they'll have to change it to recreation and then they might be satisfied. They say that spring practice fills the boys with too much football. After seeing a Florida State team play in the fall, would you say they lacked competitive desire?

"The next argument hurled against football is the evil effects of intersectional games. Critics maintain that these games give football entirely too much importance, that they take too much time from classroom work, that in order to correct this fault, schedules should be confined to traditional rivals in a college's own section. Some even went so far as to say that the number of games should be cut down to four. Better yet, to one, so more time could be given to intramural and interclass football. This sort of loose, uninformed talk really upsets me.

"At Florida State, we probably have the best organized intramural system in the country. Each fall, there are dormitory, sorority, independent and fraternity teams competing against one another for championship honors. And on each team there are about thirty people. Is this a new idea they're trying to put across? Heck no, this program of ours has been going along but for thirty years and I suppose it seems peculiar to some of them that we're still able to carry on a varsity schedule. In the entire fall travel, we only missed two class days.

"Apparently, these reformers are taking a slap at intersectional football because it has been a very important asset to the game. Centuries ago the countries of the Balkan states competed annually in what are supposed to be the original Olympic Games. During that period when the boys from the different countries of Turkey, Greece, etc., competed in these games, they had a chance to become acquainted, to exchange ideas, and to cement a more friendly relationship. Any Grecian propaganda concerning one of the competing countries was quickly quelled because their representatives understood one another's ideas and customs. In that time, there was little or no warfare. Two thousand years ago these games were stopped and the Balkan states became a hotbed of revolution. In October, 1880, however, some farsighted moderators saw the necessity of resuming these games. This move has done more to eliminate warfare among these states than anything in its history. They are all now on peaceful terms.

"The United States is supposed to be a closely knit union. We are supposed to work in smooth harmony. Is there any better way to exchange our ideas than by means of athletic contests of intersectional variety? Our younger generation is to be the future governing body, legislators and citizens. Do you mean to tell me that they are not getting the right start for these duties by meeting these boys from other parts?

"Variety is itself a great education. The guys have a chance to meet and make new friends with their opponents. They come in contact with new ideas. They lose old prejudices. If someone should say to them that the California people are narrow-minded, they can stand up and attack that statement. They learn that all Southerners are not lazy, that all Northerners are not cold-blooded, and that all Mid-westerners are not all hicks. They get a slant on every part of the country, a brushing up against every type of personality. It gives them a broader and better view of life and people.

No, there's nothing wrong with intersectional football. Get out of your own back yard and get going is what I say. These young men came to college to get an education. What better way can they get it than by such contact? Intersectional games also give the alumni of these sections closer contact with their alma mater. They can't come to see their college team, so their college team comes to see them. It builds up dormant pride in their colleges, proves to their friends the truth of their loyal statements about that college, demonstrates the type of boy now attending, and gives parents a chance to see something representative of the college where they intend to enroll their children.

"Too much publicity and space given to college football in the newspapers is the third mooted question. Again let me give some answers to their arguments lined up for a quick release.

"Can I help it if the public of the United States prefers to read about clean competitive sports rather than corrupt politics and brutal murders? The circulation managers of the newspapers have their fingers at all times on the pulse of the public taste. Football, plenty about it, and that's plenty interesting—is what they demand. That's the reason they have sports writers covering the practice sessions and the games, so that their readers can keep up with the progress of their favorite teams. Usually coaches do not send for them.

They come on their own accord. And we always try to coop-
erate and give them what they want.

"It pleases the vanity of the public to read an account of
the game they have just seen. Somehow they like to see in
print what a popular sports writer had to say about a certain
end run that was pulled off, while they were watching from
the sidelines. If it tallies with their opinion, they say, 'Just
what I told you.' If it doesn't, it gives them room for an
argument. That's human nature. I assure you the football
coaches didn't think that one up.

"More people are interested in football than the spectators
in the stadium. Some of the greatest rooters have to set at
home or work. If they can't get the game by radio or television, they read about it in the newspaper, filling in with their
imaginations between the lines of print describing the game,
play-by-play. They like to study the photographs of the
players and plays. When they see the game a few days later
on a replay, they like to relive their original vacarious excitement, or try to figure out the play they didn't see.

"The main reason colleges send out advance publicity
from the athletic department to the newspapers is because
the public wants it. They want to figure out just how their
team's chances are shaping up for the coming Saturday, what
this or that player is expected to do, or if any surprise plays
are in the offering, they want to be warned to look out for
them. The only way they can keep up to the minute is to
follow the columns of the sports pages.

"In an interview made last winter with a well known college coach it was mentioned in passing that college football
was under-commercialized rather than overcommercialized.
Some young reporter, looking for a back door to momentary
prominence, threw a light upon the subject entirely different
from that which had been intended. The coach replied in saying that comparatively few of the schools are making money
out of football, that all of this criticism is directed at a few
big schools that have played to large crowds and have
naturally reaped a big money harvest.

"In the game of football, our team is tested on eleven autumn Saturdays and whether we pass, or not, is judged by fifty thousand fans."

BOWDEN!

"But what about the other schools throughout the country that are not able to meet expenses and are losing money? The coach then asked, 'You read in the newspapers everyday about some school in trouble, or one has dropped their program because they are financially unable to carry it on. Some of the big powers are even having it tough like Colorado for an example.

"So what is over-commercialization in football? Of course, some of the schools play to big crowds. Where does the money go? Does the faculty get it? Do the football coaches benefit by it? Does it go into the hands of alumni? No, it does not. Most of it goes into the college treasury to help build new facilities such as dormitories, buildings, and better recreational facilities, so that the college might be better able to give the student body a more complete education. The amount of money that is left in the athletic treasury helps to carry the other varsity sports as well as the intramural program. If schools don't have big crowds at their varsity games, how are they going to carry on the other and broader athletic activities? Very few sports are on a paying basis, and nationally they look to football receipts for help; it just means if schools try to cut down on the crowds, that they will have to cut down on all their other sports, which will prevent thousands of college boys from getting the physical development that usually comes with his education.

"Let me go on. No, there's nothing wrong with football, nor any phase of it. The 'anti-football men' like to take a crack at it every now and then just because it is successful. A prominent man remarked to me one time that as long as people critize you, it's a sure sign that you're getting along well. Their denunciations are so silly and so utterly without a sound basis that it is foolish for us to even argue their points. Suppose the football coaches should walk into their offices and tear apart their staffs and tell them to cut down on overhead. I wonder what their reaction to this would be? Yet, we're supposed to sit quietly by and swallow whatever comes into their minds and like it. Football is a great game. If there's any harm coming from it, it's coming from the crowds who insist on flocking into the stadium, so why blame football? It's like the man with indigestion blaming the food instead of himself for overeating. Football is around to stay and at Florida State—I hope it lasts forever!"

22

The Game Plan

In Bobby Bowden's winning football play-book, there is a fundamental philosophy that makes a strong comparison between the game of football and the game of life. To Bowden, the ingredients that are used to make winning teams can also be applied to a winning walk with the real Head Coach, Jesus Christ. Bowden feels very strongly about this philosophy and this writer has developed the following outline based on Bowden's lifestyle which, hopefully, can be used in developing one's own daily "game plan."

1. Set your Priorities

Prayer is a very important aspect of a young man's life. Finding time for prayer is simply a matter of setting your priorities. Nearly everyone has the same amount of time in a twenty-four-hour day. Therefore, one's use and management of time depends upon one's system of values. Whatever one deems of greatest importance will have priority. Almost everyone takes time to eat, sleep, and observe the ordinary demands of daily living. Most have the responsibility of a gainful occupation or profession. The duties and responsibilities of homemaking and parenting, in spite of all our modern conveniences, are definitely most time consuming for most adults. Even so, a disciplined management of time will make possible a life of daily devotion and prayer that is deeply rewarding.

2. Be Organized

Everybody has 168 hours in a week except football coaches. They have 198. Yet if we put them aside and consider that the average person works 40 hours on the job, 128 hours remain in the week. And if we allow 56 hours (eight good hours a day) for sleep, that still leaves 72 hours.

Now, we've got to remember eating, so discount 21 hours per week for meals, which reduces the balance to 51 hours. All of these activities seem irrevocably necessary. Yet, taking from that balance a minimum of thirty minutes per day for a "quiet time" of scripture reading and prayer, one still has over 47 hours a week for unanticipated and unprogrammed activities. This hypothetical program, of course, does not apply to housewives and farmers, that I know. It is only an attempt to illustrate that disciplined management of time and a properly organized system of priorities can make possible at least a minimal devotional life.

3. Prepare a "Game Plan"

In most prayer programs, the midweek prayer service in many churches is only a starter. This, of course, can be supplemented by various prayer meetings where the time is conscientiously given to prayer. Excellent examples of these gatherings are women's prayer luncheons, men's prayer breakfasts, the Fellowship of Christian Athletes and Athletes in Action huddle groups, and school assemblies.

Also, it is better to begin with a small program that can be maintained and increased than to plunge into too heavy a program and flounder. These programs may be formulated into weekly meetings much like our Fellowship of Christian Athletes huddle group at Florida State.

4. Give the Credit or the Blame to the Head Coach

On the Florida State football team there are no real heroes because the players play with a team concept. After the game the newspaper and players always give the credit or the failure to the head coach, which is the way it should be.

I firmly believe that the quality of a young man's life is in direct proportion to his commitment to excellence.

Therefore, on God's team shouldn't the praise be passed on to the Master Coach?

But why Praise? Until recently, we've had more teaching on prayer and very little on praise. Yet, there is much more emphasis in the Bible on praise than prayer. A fine example of this is Psalm 145:10 . . . *"All thy works shall praise thee."*

And if the highest function of the angelic host is praise, it follows logically that the highest function of the human spirit should also be praise. Ever-increasing approximation to the infinitely lovely character of God is the most sublime goal of all creation. This is the *summer blossom*, the greatest good, the highest joy, the most exquisite delight, the supreme rapture, and the most ravishing transport of the human spirit. Just as antagonism, hostility, and cursing against God exercise and strengthen all that is most abominable, diabolical, and base in the human spirit, so worship and praise of the infinite God exercise, reinforce, and strengthen all that is most sublime, transcendent, and divine in the human being. Thus, as one worships and praises, he is continually transformed step by step, from glory to glory, into the image of the infinitely happy God. And the process can be expected to continue eternally. Therefore, praise is the most useful occupation and activity in enabling God to realize the supreme goal of the universe, that of "bringing many unto glory."

5. Consider the kind of team member you should be

Since football is a team sport, it is very important for each player and coach to realize his contribution to the team. A fine example is that of the Christian coach who became the Head Coach at a new school and immediately began hiring his assistant coaches with the policy of hiring only Christians. However, it took him but one season to change that practice. His reason was that the believers he hired didn't do a good job.

"I can't figure it out," the coach finally commented. "It must be that since salvation is free, they assume that everything else is too."

Not a very good commentary on the lifestyle of people who are supposed to be committed to the Lord, is it? It's the same attitude that Jesus was speaking of when He asked a group of His followers, *"Why do you call me, 'Lord, Lord; and do not do what I say?" (Luke 6:46)* A disobedient Christian is a contradiction in terms. And what you say about Christ being your Lord has got to be how you live. Righteousness, therefore, is doing what is right.

6. The Little Things

So often, I find Coach Bowden discussing the primary importance of the *little things*. And he is so right, because it's the little things that can get you beaten both on the football field, or in life.

Once, a man of God from Judeah was sent to King Jeroboam with a message that God was going to judge the king for his wickedness. When Jeroboam pointed at the man of God with a command that he be thrown into prison, the hand he had stretched out just drew up. God's power was obviously with this prophet.

But there was one problem. The man of God had strict orders from the Lord not to eat bread or drink water in that place. When the King offered these things to him, he refused in no uncertain terms. But as he was going home, another prophet stopped him and announced that God had made a later revelation that it was all right for him to eat and drink there after all, and he invited the man of God to his house.

The second prophet was older and, of course, wisdom and age go together, don't they? Our man of God obviously thought so, because without even asking God, he went with the man. In return from his disobedience, God had him torn apart by a lion.

The *little things* usually don't matter that much to us but they matter a great deal to God. Paul the Apostle understood this, and declared that his goal was *"to maintain always a blameless conscience both before God and before man."* (Acts 26:16)

7. Your Bread and Butter Play

In every playbook of a football team in America, you'll always find a *bread and butter play*, the kind of play that will always be a consistent 4- to 5-yard gainer. I know that at Florida State where they use the passing game a lot, Coach Bowden will instruct his quarterback to call the quick-out pass play on nearly every crucial 3rd down situation because it's so effective.

Among Christians you'll find a variety of responses to the Bible. Some describe it as caster oil—bitter, but good for what ails you; then there's the Shredded Wheat approach—

"Teaching young men that what they learn in football can be applied to the game of life is an important goal."

"The 'little things' in a young man's life are very important for him to become a winner."

it's dry, but nourishing; or there are those who use it like Brylcream—a little dab'll do ya.

However, it's next to impossible to build a life of true faith without the Bible, because the Bible keeps you in touch with the resources of God. Faith without the Bible to guide it is like a destitute man who's found out that his family fortune is buried somewhere in the Appalachian Mountains. He might be able to get the money eventually by digging here and there, but how much easier would it be if he'd just had a map.

Paul the Apostle says, *"Faith comes from hearing, and hearing by the Word of God."* (Romans 10:17)

8. Winning in the Fourth Quarter

Coach Bowden is a master at arousing the deep-being of his players during fourth quarter crises and then leading them to victory. And "Winning in the Fourth Quarter" is one of his key slogans. He is a firm believer that if a youngster can come back in the fourth quarter to win a game, then he can face any difficult situation placed before him in later life.

This same "fourth quarter" situation applies off the field with Chrisitans, too. Christ knew this and thus prepared a game plan for us to follow.

If the exalted Lord Jesus Christ received us in our unlovely status, should we not likewise welcome the unacceptable?

> *Did you ever stop to think*
> *How lonely God would be*
> *If the only folks He loved*
> *Were those as good as He?*

During Christ's ministry He rubbed shoulders with rich rulers and poor widows. He accepted invitations to dinner at the home of the self-righteous Pharisee Simon and the penitent publican Matthew. He fellowshipped with adults and took babies and children in His arms. Multitudes moved Him to compassion and He had time for interviews with the individual. A large share of Christ's energies were devoted to the sick, while He still showed concern for the healthy. He paid attention to both white-collared lawyers and menial fisher-men. His wide scope of influence was foreshadowed in His infancy when poor shepherds and rich Magi came to adore Him. Yet like a true "winner," He handled it in stride. But winners are like that.

9. After the Game

On eleven autumn Saturdays for sixty minutes of a game, head coach Bobby Bowden and the FSU gang play the best brand of football in America. However, their off-the-field activities account for the bulk of their calendar year and these are the most important times of their young lives. Hal Hayes, sports writer of the *Birmingham News* and a fine Christian, once gave a brilliant description of Jeff Rutledge, Christian quarterback at the University of Alabama during his senior season in 1978.

"In the locker room you consider yourself a mere answering service for compliments. You take them, sure, and you smile brightly. Then you pass them along to The One you know in your heart they truly belong.

"You've worked hard and winning on Saturday would be the fulfillment of many dreams. But a thing called Ultimate Victory is what you're really striving for.

"You've said you're playing for Somebody Else, a higher being—a richer reward—and because of it, your life's been blessed.

"A man called Jesus is the central figure in your life. You've long said you just want to be judged a winner in His eyes.

"And after all, that's the measure that really counts.

"*I'm giving you the ball, son, and naming you quarterback for your team in the game of life. It is a long game with no time outs and no substitutions.*

"*You'll have a great backfield with great reputations. They are named Faith, Hope and Love. You'll work behind a truly powerful line. End to end, it consists of honesty, loyalty, devotion to duty, self-respect, study, cleanliness and good behavior.*

"The goal is the Gates of Heaven. God is the referee and sole official. There are ten rules. You know them as the Ten Commandments.

"The ball, it is your immortal soul. Hold on to it. Now, son, get in there and see what you can do with it!"

About the Author

Mike Bynum is a senior at The University of Alabama, New College Division. He is a pre-law student, majoring in English and has a quality point average of 2.3 on a 3.0 scale.

During his first 3 years at Alabama, Mike served as a student manager for Coach Paul Bryant and the Crimson Tide football team. In that three year period, Alabama won 31 games, lost 5, including bowl game wins over UCLA in the Liberty Bowl, and Penn State and Ohio State in the Sugar Bowl. Currently, Mike is a member of the Fellowship of Christian Athletes, a Dean's List Student, President of the New College Division of The University of Alabama, a Diamond Century Club member at Texas A&M, a Gold Club member at the University of Mississippi, and has been recently elected to the Who's Who Among American Colleges and Universities.

BOUND FOR GLORY is his sixth book. Mike's first book, HIGH TIDE is the story of the Alabama Crimson Tide, on the road to the national championship. BRYANT . . . THE MAN THE MYTH, Mike's second book, is a walk down memory lane with the greatest coach in America, Paul "Bear" Bryant, and his successful coaching career at Maryland, Kentucky, Texas A&M, and Alabama. His third book, NEVER SAY QUIT, is the miraculous story of Alabama quarterback Steadman Shealy as he came back from knee surgery to lead his team to national championships in 1978 and 1979. AGGIE PRIDE, Mike's fourth book, is the story of Texas A&M football under winning coaches Bryant, Stallings, Bellard and Wilson. WE BELIEVE, his fifth book, is the story of Coach Bryant's greatest players and how they became great men later in life.

Currently, Mike has plans for one more book, GOLDEN GLORY, a collaborative effort with Al Wester on the great 1946-49 Notre Dame teams.

Photo Credits

South Georgia College

Samford University Information Services

West Virginia University Sports Information Office

Florida State University Sports Information Office

The Birmingham News

The Tallahassee Democrat

Appendix

THE BOWDEN RECORD

Woodlawn High; Birmingham, Alabama

> Team Captain, 1948
> > All City, 1948
> > All State, 1948

University of Alabama; Tuscaloosa, Alabama

> Athletic Grant-in-Aid, 1949

Howard College; Birmingham, Ala.

> Team Captain, 1952
> > All-Dixie, 1950, 1951, 1952
> > All-America, 1952

ΠΚΑ All-America

Georgia Junior College Champions, 1955, 1956, 1957

Georgia Junior College Coach of the Year, 1955, 1957

Blue-Gray Game, Head Coach, Blue Team, 1970

All-America Bowl, South, 1976

Japan Bowl, 1977

Associated Press Southern Independent
Coach of the Year, 1977, 1979

Division I Coach of the Year, 1979

BOWDEN'S RECORD AS HEAD COACH

Won 129, Lost 55, Tied 1

Year	School	W	L	T
1955	South Georgia	6	3	0
1956	South Georgia	5	3	0
1957	South Georgia	6	3	0
1958	South Georgia	5	2	1
1959	Howard College	* 9	1	0
1960	Howard College	8	1	0
1961	Howard College	7	2	0
1962	Howard College	* 7	2	0
1970	West Virginia	8	3	0
1971	West Virginia	7	4	0
1972	West Virginia	* 8	4	0
1973	West Virginia	6	5	0
1974	West Virginia	4	7	0
1975	West Virginia	* 9	3	0
1976	Florida State	5	6	0
1977	Florida State	*10	2	0
1978	Florida State	8	3	0
1979	Florida State	*11	1	0

*Bowl Games

1959—Textile Bowl, Howard 52, Gordon Military 20
1962—Golden Isle Bowl, McNeese State 21, Howard 14
1972—Peach Bowl, N.C. State 49, West Virginia 13
1975—Peach Bowl, West Virginia 13, N.C. State 10
1977—Tangerine Bowl, Florida State 40, Texas Tech 17
1980—Orange Bowl, Oklahoma 24, Florida State 7